WOMEN'S
GUIDE TO
OVERSEAS LIVING

Second Edition

Women's
Guide to
Overseas Living

Second Edition

Nancy J. Piet-Pelon • Barbara Hornby

Intercultural Press, Inc.

For information, contact:
Intercultural Press, Inc.
P.O. Box 700
Yarmouth, Maine 04096, USA

Cover Design: Letterspace
Interior Design: Patty J. Topel

Printed in the United States of America

97 96 95 94   4 5 6 7

Library of Congress Cataloging-in-Publication Data
Piet-Pelon, Nancy J. and Barbara Hornby
    Women's Guide to Overseas Living
    Revised Edition of: In Another Dimension. 1st ed. 1985.
        p. cm.
    Includes bibliographical references.
    ISBN 1-877864-05-6
    1. Women—United States—Handbooks, manuals, etc. 2. Americans—
Foreign countries—Handbooks, manuals, etc. 3. Intercultural communication—Handbooks, manuals, etc. In Another Dimension. III. Title.
305.4—dc20
                                        92-40422
                                        CIP

Contents

Preface to the First Edition

Vagabonds, adventurers, strangers, aliens, expatriates, dependents, wanderers, pioneers. So many names for people who choose to live overseas. Novels have often portrayed them as young men in search of adventure who return as old, weather-beaten wags with an endless supply of romantic stories. There were also, of course, the conquistadores and colonial administrators of the age of empire building. But the world has changed since then, as have those who decide to spend significant portions of their lives overseas.

Living abroad is more pragmatic now and perhaps more mundane. People go overseas to fulfill a contract or, perhaps, two. They are called multinational businessmen, technocrats, consultants, liaison officers. They wear business suits, diplomatic garb or hard hats. They may be seeking adventure, but more likely they seek promotions, career benefits, larger salaries, or a more comfortable lifestyle.

Women have been part of the overseas scene for almost as long as men, helping them wield colonial power or engaging in the "good work" of missionaries. Women went where their husbands did, occasionally seeking hill stations in the heat but basically being stalwart and dependable.

Is it the same today? Not really. Women are involved in their own lives. They do not move without question to further a husband's career. Whether women have changed is not the issue. The times are different. Women have their own educational experiences, their own careers, and their own identities.

Moving overseas means a big change in a woman's life. It is our intent in this book to examine the kinds of changes today's women encounter when moving abroad and what can be done about them.

Each of the authors chose, some years ago, to accompany her husband overseas wherever career opportunities arose for him. Our paths crossed in Indonesia in 1981. By then we had lived in many places. Barbara made her first cross-cultural adjustments as the American wife of a British citizen living in England. From there they moved to India, then to Nepal, and finally to Indonesia. For Nancy, the wanderlust of her India-born American husband took her to Indonesia in 1970, then to Bangladesh, Pakistan, and Egypt, before a happy return to Indonesia in 1980. We had managed to adjust, but we still felt the challenge of living overseas. We also wanted to explore the other options to the path we had taken. Finally, we wanted to see if we could help other women in the process of adjustment and in exploring options.

We were poorly prepared for our cross-cultural living. As a result, we missed too much that we might have enjoyed, and we wanted to help other women take advantage of the opportunities available to them. Yet this is not a book of magical solutions. We do not presume that much! Rather, it is a book of shared experiences, ours plus those of the many women we have met along the way. We have chosen to write this book because we believe that cross-cultural living is one of life's great experiences, adding an extra dimension to it.

We have been enriched by this project and by the women who helped us. Some have shared their experiences; others have helped with practical suggestions. Some provided the encouragement to keep us going; others gave technical assistance on various chapters. It has not been easy to complete this book with one of us in Asia and the other in England. Had it not been for our friends on both sides of the world, we could not have done it. We thank them all and mention by name those who made special contributions. But first of all, David Hoopes's meticulous work on the manuscript deserves our thanks. His contributions were many, but we particularly appreciate his assistance in developing the section on culture shock in Chapter 5.

In Indonesia: Maureen Allgrove, Kurie Alim, Jeanne Blumberg, Lorna Burke, Judith Chaplin, Paula Hart, Barbara Macrae, Phung O'Riordan, Tuti Rahardjo, Sarah Roberts, Soejatni, Pam Straley, Rosanne Walters, the Comprehensive Orientation Program staff of the International Community Activities Center, and the Indonesian Allied Medical Association members.

In other parts of the world: Maria Breetveld, Julianne Fraser Facknitz, Chloe Greaves, Elizabeth Sidney, and Sylvia Spaven.

The men in our lives also deserve special mention. To David Piet and Peter Hornby our special thanks for making it all happen. Without them we would not have had the experiences to write about nor the encouragement to see it through. Michael Piet made it fun, and even at the age of six, understood our need for quiet!

Nancy J. Piet-Pelon   Barbara Hornby
Jakarta, Indonesia   Upper Boddington, England

Preface to the Second Edition

Since publication of the first edition of this book in 1985—which at the time was entitled *In Another Dimension*—globalization has accelerated, drawing the people of the world even closer together. Travel; communication; economic and educational exchange; and the global movement of refugees, immigrants, guest workers, skilled professionals, and business executives have all contributed to this process, making the world seem even smaller than it was only eight years ago. More important for this book, however, is the changing role of women in the globalization process. Their role is more critical than it was, and our understanding of what women need to know to manage effectively as expatriates has increased significantly.

For these reasons and a number of others, we decided there was a need for a second edition of our book. Fortunately, the Intercultural Press agreed, and its editors encouraged us to make the necessary revisions. We have added a chapter on reentry to one's home culture and one addressing special concerns: discrimination, being from a relatively unknown country, being a foreign-born spouse, and expecting more similarities than differences in the host culture. We have also added new sections to existing chapters, providing updated information on problems arising from marital estrangement and divorce, on terrorism, and on women who work.

The title has also changed. We feel *Women's Guide to Overseas Living* better reflects the content of the book. *In An-*

other Dimension, while rather intriguing, was mistaken by many people for a science fiction novel!

A number of friends and colleagues have helped us with this new edition. We would like to thank especially Alice Cahill in London, the members of the Women's Discussion Group of Kathmandu, the staff of the U.S. State Department Family Liaison Office and the "3 Marys" (Chatwin, Haour-Knipe and MacKinnon) of Geneva for their constructive suggestions, support and enthusiasm.

We thank again the men in our lives for their constant encouragement and sense of adventure which they pass on to us and hope that we share.

Nancy J. Piet-Pelon   Barbara Hornby
Dhaka, Bangladesh   Upper Boddington, England

Introduction

Millions of people from all over the world live in countries or cultures other than their own. Large numbers of them are men in business, development assistance, and government who pursue their careers abroad. With them are wives and children who may or may not share their career dedication.

Yet because of the importance of family and personal relationships, the wives agree to accompany them. In addition, increasingly larger numbers of women, both single and with dependents, are leaving their own cultures to work abroad.

Whether a woman follows her husband overseas or goes to pursue her own career, she will be uprooted. She will leave all that is familiar to her—her family, her neighborhood, her language, her culture and an array of intangibles which provide daily support. She will have to cope with a variety of feelings, including both excitement and apprehension about going. In *With Our Consent?* a powerful book on the subject of expatriate life written by the Geneva Women's Cooperative in 1983, the authors put it this way:

> By agreeing to relocate, those of us who travel as dependents indicate our openness to the possibilities of both greater individuation and greater alienation. By consenting to live as foreigners and potentially unemployed workers, we declare ourselves ready to sever the indigenous channels through which individuals contribute to their nations. By relinquishing all those familiar niches that together provide us with a sense of

place, purpose, and continuity in exchange for relentlessly shift-
ing constellations of people and events in an unimaginable future, we give notice that we are truly "modern" women.[1]

On arrival in the foreign country, a woman may be overwhelmed by new emotions: anxiety if she cannot communicate, fear of getting lost in unfamiliar streets, and loneliness.
She will be under pressure to succeed since most sending organizations are not interested in women who fail to adjust,
either as wives or workers. For the wife and mother, there
will be the strain of maintaining the calm and normality expected of her by her family. She may flounder as she searches
for personal identity.

Homemakers who are uprooted experience a special set
of circumstances. Unlike their husbands, they do not have an
established situation awaiting them. They are not affiliated
with an office where the work is familiar, where there is some
level of acceptance, and where there are workmates to help
them succeed because they are needed. The only people who
need homemakers, at least at first, are their husbands and
children.

Women who go overseas to work do, like men, have
support in the work setting. Yet they are still uprooted and
will normally experience culture shock. In addition they may
be subject to prejudice in countries where local women do not
pursue professional careers or even leave the home to work.
Quoting again from *With Our Consent?* as Geneva is discussed:

> Women who arrive as privileged foreign wives must reconcile
> the abstract, "universal" principles of equality and justice . . .
> with the contradictory realities found in both the host culture
> and the international milieu. As world citizens they are ex-

---

[1] Geneva Women's Cooperative, *With Our Consent?* (Geneva: Geneva
Women's Cooperative, 1983).

pected to become knowledgeable about the global goals for women . . . and at the same time, to exempt themselves from the process of actively pursuing these goals in this setting.[2]

Those familiar with the challenges of overseas living know that many people return home before completing their contracts, often because the family was not adequately prepared. They recommend orientation programs which deal with such things as expectations, culture shock, household management and daily life overseas. They stress the importance of providing orientation for the whole family, not just the breadwinner. They increasingly advocate some sort of preselection testing to see if the worker and his or her spouse can live and work effectively in another culture.

They know the high costs of relocation. Sending organizations therefore have a strong economic incentive to prepare the *whole* family for a successful international experience.

There is no question that preselection testing and orientation programs can ease transition. Yet we have found that there are several other factors adversely affecting adjustment which orientation programs do not magically erase. They cannot, for example, create a place for the women who move into a new post with no formal role.

The number of women who have their own careers is also rapidly growing. When we wrote in the early 1980s about women pursuing their own careers overseas, we were talking about a minority. That is no longer true. More and more women are going overseas on their own, with husbands as dependents or *sans* husband but with children whom they must continue to nurture while following their career. In short, women overseas reflect the demographic and sociocultural changes which have occurred in all the developed countries of the world. They are climbing career ladders, making

[2] Ibid.

the shifts to managerial positions, placing career decisions before those of family and long-term relationships.

The United States Agency for International Development (USAID) mission to Nepal offers a microcosmic view of the picture repeated throughout the world. The director is a bachelor, his deputy a married man with a wife who pursues her own career as a librarian at each of their posts. The secretary is half of a tandem (dual-career) couple; her husband runs the executive/management branch of USAID. The economist is a single woman. In each of the technical offices, the pattern is repeated—men engage in their work while their wives work as consultants in other development agencies or pursue their careers through voluntary work.

We also see a shift among women who carry on the roles of wife and mother. Fewer are willing to remain in the role of *dependent* spouse. Instead, they are seeking positions in their own right, wherever they live.

These changes have caused frustrations for many women who are often confounded by the employment rules and regulations governing "dependent" wives within the country where they reside. The decision to work or not is often not theirs to make. And even if they manage to successfully negotiate the morass of regulations, they often run afoul of customs which preclude women from working outside the home.

More families are consequently seeking alternative lifestyles. Women stay in the home country with the children, following their careers, while their husbands live alone in the foreign country. The U.S. Foreign Service recognizes this problem by providing assistance (on a case-by-case basis) for couples who have to keep two homes because one of them chooses to stay in the home country to follow her (or his) career, or for other reasons such as the children's education or the care of elderly parents.

Another factor which has become more important since the first edition of this book was published is that of the rising costs of maintaining families overseas. Oil companies in particular are finding it more economical to structure some of their jobs so that the employee is not accompanied abroad by family. While the spouse stays in the home country, the worker travels to oil fields to work on a three-months-on/one-month-off arrangement. The family members never visit the country where the breadwinner is working, thus risking feelings of alienation among family members and difficulties for the worker who lacks personal support while working under trying conditions.

The least amount of change has taken place in the length of tours in many overseas positions. In spite of the increasing recognition that it may take six months to adjust after arrival and another six months to prepare mentally and physically for the next posting or for the return home, some governments, corporations, and organizations still enforce a two- or even one-year limit on some assignments, usually to places considered to be "hardship" posts. The result is that the family has only a short time (or no time) in which to be really effective, and the chances of finding satisfying work for the spouse are negligible, particularly in the very countries considered to be hardship posts. After a few such tours, ennui sets in and many families no longer bother to adjust at all to new surroundings but frequent the expatriate clubs where they do not have to make an effort.

In this book we try to speak to the needs of all types of women who are going overseas. Though each of us is unique, we have found that there are enough similarities in our lives to develop sound guidelines for moving abroad, adjusting to a new environment, and enjoying the process. It is essential to be prepared. Enough women have gone overseas through the years that none of us need feel she is navigating uncharted waters. We have attempted to distill this accumulated knowledge and wisdom into guidelines which will help you prepare for your overseas experience. Among other things, we will look at what you need to do to prepare yourself; help you analyze your motives; acquaint you with culture shock and the adjustment process; discuss the special problems of women in the home and in the workplace; and offer practical suggestions on handling your children, organizing your household, staying healthy, and managing stress. We will help you cope with reentry, a subject we did not include in the first edition. This omission has now been rectified because so many women have told us that going home caused the greatest pain and was the time when they needed guidance. When women are unable to make a successful reentry, or fail to guide their children through it with a minimum of scars, the entire overseas experience becomes negatively tainted.

The authors have lived primarily in the developing countries of Asia. It will be apparent as you read that our orientation is toward the experience of living in those countries. Nevertheless, we believe strongly that most of what we say is applicable not only in developing countries but—with some obvious exceptions such as dealing with live-in household help and managing health problems—in Western countries as well.

In this second edition we have responded to comments on the first edition by adding a section on women living and working in Europe. Many women do not move as far from home as the authors did, but the alienation they feel is just as acute. We have come to realize that the shock of moving to another Western country can be as difficult to cope with as that of moving to a place where it is immediately obvious that we are strangers. In Bonn, a blond, blue-eyed Briton gets no notice on the street. Because she does not look different, when she needs help or cannot find her way and cannot communicate, no help is forthcoming; the feeling of alienation is acute. If the same person were lost on a street in Jakarta, she would be noticed. While possibly not always appreciating the attention, she knows that help is possible simply because she looks different.

When we first wrote this book, we did so, quite naturally, from the perspective of women from large and/or influential countries. Women from smaller countries have pointed out to us that we were writing from a position of cultural strength and recognized power. Wherever we go it is likely that our countries (Britain and the United States) are well known—as are the products of our cultures such as pop singers and soft drinks. This is not so for our fellow sojourners from smaller and less prominent countries. As one Swedish friend in Nepal said after reading *In Another Dimension,*

> You failed us. You do not understand what it is like to find no one who has heard of your country. You can always find someone who speaks your language. Even if they speak it badly, it is still *your* language. We don't have that luxury. It seems no one here has even heard of Sweden, and they certainly don't know our language or anything about our culture. I think that makes it harder for us to adjust.

Another difficult issue is that of being black in countries in Asia and Latin America. In Asia, especially, black is definitely not beautiful. Many of the demons of Hindu mythology are black and ghosts of fairy tales are depicted with black faces. There is also prejudice against Western blacks who travel to sub-Saharan Africa, where their status, not their color, sets them apart.

A third issue concerns women who are half of an interracial or intercultural marriage. Though it is no longer unusual to find couples who have married across formerly forbidden lines, theirs is still a unique and often difficult position. An Asian bride who has not yet adjusted to her new American family before she is taken into another cultural situation will have a whole different set of adjustments to make. The Association of American Foreign Service Women has an active group of "foreign-born spouses" who assist this growing group of women. We have drawn on them for pertinent information. All of these issues have been included in this second edition in the chapter, "Special Concerns."

Though we have conducted many interviews and been involved in seminars, orientation programs, and personal counseling, this book is not based on questionnaires and statistical data. It is confirmed by other research, however. Julianne Fraser Facknitz, in a thesis written a number of years ago and based on interviews with transnational women in New Delhi and Geneva, came to the same conclusions we have: that life overseas, for all of its benefits, places incredible strains on women.

> Without a doubt there is glamour in Istanbul and many other faraway places. It is a rare individual, however, who is sustained by the excitement of a new place through years of transnational living. On the contrary, transnationals need to be studied because they are subject to problems. They go to live in countries other than their own and suddenly realize that they are foreigners. They probably considered themselves mature and competent, and suddenly they feel like children again, unable to cope with a new language and with dozens of different ways of performing mundane chores.[3]

Only in recent years have sending organizations paid more than lip service to the special issues which face women who move overseas. There have been books on the problems of cross-cultural communication, doing business or raising children overseas (see the Bibliography) but none dealing with the broad range of issues concerning women.

This was true when we wrote the first edition, and we find that little has changed over the years, both with regard to the attitudes of sending organizations and in the availability of books on the subject. That is why we have written this second edition. We encourage women, wherever they live, to examine their feelings, both positive and negative, about living overseas and to speak out. As we said in the first edition, the time to let organizations know what it is "really like" to live overseas is *now* and this is still true.

Finally, this edition is enriched by the experience we have had in our lives during the intervening years. In unique ways,

---

[3] Julianne Fraser Facknitz, *Transitional Women: A Study in Cross-cultural Relations,* thesis, Goddard College, 1978.

we exemplify the changes that have occurred among women who have thrown their lot in with their traveling husbands. Barbara and Peter have chosen to return to England to set up their own consulting business, but their eyes are still turned toward the world as they consult in areas as far flung as Ghana and the Solomon Islands.

Nancy, David, and Michael have lived in their home country briefly, resided in the fabled Himalayan Kingdom of Nepal, and are now living and working in Bangladesh. After years of living in Indonesia, where modernization was the rule rather than the exception, Nancy had to slow to the pace of Nepal. She also had to adjust to being unable to work there and had to go to Bangladesh, Ghana, and Indonesia to pursue her profession.

Our aim in writing this second edition is the same as it was in writing the first. We are still trying, as Facknitz has simply stated, to "shed light on what it really means to live outside one's own culture, so that the negative effects may be ameliorated and the positive ones emphasized."[4]

---

[4] Ibid.

one

Matters of Culture

The different cultures of the world and the people who constitute them are thrust toward each other at a fearful pace. The cultures we come from deeply affect our thinking and our ways of behaving, our "personhood." The cultures to which we move are often steeped in traditions radically different from our own. It is in this contact and confrontation that cultures as a whole experience the shock of rapid change in the modern world and the individual experiences culture shock. These two ideas, *culture shock* and *cultures in shock,* are briefly explored in this chapter in order to provide a framework for understanding why guidance is needed for entering a new culture. These are not matters, however, which are learned once and then forgotten. They come back to us again and again, whether on the first move overseas or the tenth.

CULTURE SHOCK

Perhaps during the time you are preparing to move overseas, a well-meaning friend will say (often with a slight touch of malicious glee) "You're in for a real shock when you get to _____ !" A shock? The thought may scare you. But it also raises questions. What kind of shock? How will it affect your adjustment and that of the family?

Many people going abroad do not believe they will experience culture shock, an attitude that prevents them from hearing unpleasant information and dealing constructively with the feelings they have when culture shock occurs. After all, they will say, we have not become so spoiled that insufficient electricity, germs in the water, spicy foods, or the lack of supermarkets will disturb us. They cannot believe that the shock people refer to runs far deeper than we can imagine from our comfortable home base. Yet we all learn that culture shock is very real. Everyone experiences it in some way in each new culture and country to which he or she goes—and, normally, upon returning home.

Culture can be defined in many ways. For the purpose of this book culture is defined as follows: all the ways of living which have been developed by a group of human beings and which are transmitted from one generation to another. But culture is not taught like reading, writing and arithmetic. No one sits a child down and says, "Now it is time to learn culture." Rather it is learned through a process of observing, doing, and being told how to behave in specific situations. It inculcates the norms of human behavior which prevail in a society. Table manners are part of culture, as are social graces and greetings. But so are values and value-based behavior and the entire system of relationships among people. It is our culture that guides the development of relationships and defines their parameters.

In its simplest form, culture shock occurs when our cultural cues, the signs and symbols which guide social interaction, are stripped away. We embark from our home country surrounded by the warmth of love and emotion that go into fond and difficult farewells. We know how to say *good-bye* in our own culture. The shock comes in disembarking in the new country and not knowing the acceptable way to say *hello*. A difficult part of this process for adults is the experience of feeling like children again, of not knowing *instinctively* the "right" thing to do. Enormous amounts of energy must suddenly be spent on small tasks, simple social etiquette and relationship building. The stress caused by this effort is called culture shock.

Culture shock is a process that lends itself to being analyzed by stages. There are minor points of difference among the experts on these stages, but there is basic agreement on the kinds of emotions and concerns that people will have as they try to adjust to living overseas.

First comes the *honeymoon* stage when the world is seen through the rose-colored glasses of excitement and anticipation. This is followed by *anxiety,* usually brought on by settling-in problems. The next stage is *rejection* when the individual becomes hypercritical of the new culture. Some form of *regression* usually occurs next when the sojourner retreats from the situation in ways ranging from quite ordinary to rather bizarre. Finally, the *adjustment* stage begins as the person takes steps to understand and accept the new milieu.

Culture shock is discussed in greater detail in Chapter 5. The important point to remember here is that the mental and emotional stress of moving abroad—embodied in the term culture shock—should be anticipated from the beginning.

CULTURES IN SHOCK

Cultures are tradition-bound yet dynamic and subject to change over time. Those who move to a new culture may in preparation read literature from earlier times and arrive to find a culture that is quite different. In the modern world, cultures are also in shock. As one author stated,

> We live in a fantastic century. . . . We hear on all sides that East and West are meeting, but it is an understatement. They are being flung at one another with the force of atoms, the speed of jets, the restlessness of minds impatient to learn of the ways that differ from their own. From the perspective of history this may prove to be the most important fact about the twentieth century. When historians look back upon our years they may

remember them . . . as the time in which all people of the world
first had to take one another seriously.[1]

We agree with this statement. When we go overseas,
especially to developing countries, we may find some measure
of the exotic still, but the West has preceded us. The media is
there bombarding us with the news and views of the day. The
fashions, films and music that we might have happily left behind greet us on arrival. We must live with the West in a new
context and this affects our adjustment profoundly, just as it
is affecting the people we meet. Conflict and stress are apparent where countries try to match the old with the new or
throw out the old and "Westernize," often at great sacrifice.

Jakarta is an example, as are most large urban centers
throughout the developing world. In 1970, when Nancy first
went there, it was a sleepy place. It was the rare individual
who had been abroad. Everyone could tell who had a television set by the ring of people around the living room window
watching from the outside. The extended family figured
prominently in the society, with professional women depending on others to care for children while they pursued a career.
How much this has changed in two decades!

Now Jakarta is a bustling place suffering from all the
problems modernization brings to large cities. Every imagin-
able electronic gadget can be found in middle-class house-
holds. Trips to other countries are "perks" of the middle-class
government employee's job. Opportunities for study abroad
abound and are being grabbed up by both sexes. The extended
family has disintegrated in the press of urbanization because
of elderly parents fleeing the metropolis.

Jakarta is not unusual. It reflects, rather, the extent to
which societies and their cultures have changed. The breakdown of the extended family is certainly the most poignant

---

[1] Huston Smith as quoted in Ken Darrow and Brad Palmquist, eds., *Trans-
Cultural Study Guide,* 2d ed. (Palo Alto, CA: Volunteers in Asia, 1975).

example of this transition, but there are others. When we look for cultural norms, we find that our host national friends are also searching for ways to adjust their cultural heritage to their modern lifestyles. The veneer of the West is everywhere as the young people respond to the attractions of the West and disregard or reject the beauties of their own culture and the social mores of their families.

The change has come so rapidly that it leaves everyone spinning, and there is no escape from it. These changes cause both negative and positive effects. Westerners are sometimes blamed for the negative changes. If it were not for the technology of the West, often thoughtlessly brought to the East, life would go on as before—at least so the argument goes. Some yearn for the past and the simple life they remember. Yet that is not to be. Progress and development bring change and all have to be ready for what that implies. For Westerners, change has come over generations. Our cultures have had more time to adapt and grow with technological progress. For those in the societies we meet, change has been so rapid there has been little time for adjustment.

Families are under the most severe pressure. It is common for a husband to have been exposed to Western education, while the wife has not. He is comfortable in our presence. We can discuss similar problems. He knows about our country, our educational patterns, our lifestyles. He seeks us out to reinforce his new ideas, knowing that we willingly grant him sympathetic understanding. His wife is not so fortunate. She has been left behind in the Westernization process. She is out of touch with him and there is dissonance in her relationship with us. Sometimes she will resent the continuing presence of foreigners in her life; it only makes the differences between her and her husband more apparent.

Even in Western countries, the pace of change is having a radical impact. Mexico City constitutes a massive urban sprawl growing dynamically, exciting to experience, but chaotic, polluted and offering stark contrasts between poverty and wealth.

As foreigners in a new country, bridging this gap can be difficult. For women it is particularly hard. We want to know the women of our host country. They are our cultural windows. Yet when we try to approach them we are rejected. Or we are confined to discussing domestic subjects.

Nepal is a case in point. Cross-cultural parties were regular occurrences, but the social lines were clearly drawn. Women sat in one section discussing matters of the home, while the men sat in another, carrying on interesting conversations. When Barbara sat with the women, she agonized through conversations in which neither adequately spoke the other's language. Meeting the same women night after night and finding out about the children again and again was hardly stimulating. Yet crossing over to the much-envied men's group where English was the common language proved virtually impossible because of the social norms. Unless we can modify our expectations, we find ourselves smiling and nodding a great deal and wishing we were someplace else.

What can we do for our own well-being and adjustment? First we need to understand and accept the fact that the differences exist and that they can create problems. We must appreciate that the women we meet are also adjusting to us. In our own struggle for acceptance, we need to accept them. Our best intentions often fail when we move too rapidly or assume too much understanding on their part. We represent something new and the newness of that experience engenders fear, as well as interest. If we can accept that, it will help us make ourselves and our ways more understandable to others.

Many of the host country women we meet overseas, particularly in developing countries, are filled with contradictions, searching for a new identity or trying to make some sense of the West and its liberated women. Nancy once spent an evening with a group of Indonesian and American women who met to view films. These films depicted the changing roles of women in America, where liberation has brought them into competition with men and into conflict with their traditional roles. The women profiled in the films talked about their "need to work" based on self-fulfillment, personal identity, and their need for self-esteem. The older Indonesian women reacted strongly against these personal motivations. They themselves worked, but they felt they worked for the good of the family, to enhance their husband's name. They did not think it appropriate to have a personal, and what they considered selfish, motivation for working. It was not so simple for the younger Indonesian women, who were able to identify with the American ideas and could no longer accept the viewpoints of their older countrywomen. They were at odds with their own cultural values. These conflicts are a part of their lives because their own values are in transition. It is good for us to identify with these younger women, to be concerned with their struggle, and to appreciate that what they face is similar to what we have gone through.

These kinds of issues are not confined to developing countries. In Japan, women have to deal with the intricate and subtle work relationships which dominate Japanese industry and government bureaucracy. French women approach liberation in their own particular way, while feminists in Brazil confront significantly different issues.

As the world becomes a smaller place, we must recognize that by our move to a new culture, we contribute to its shrinking. We are women on the move and in transition, and as such we can have a positive effect on those we meet, confirming their sense of the need for change and comparing notes on how it can be accomplished. We can also learn, for each culture has its own special characteristics with which its women must deal. This exchange among women of the world is a major part of what moving overseas should be all about.

two

Making the Decision

Most of us would like to believe that our decision to do something of the magnitude of moving overseas is based on a long process of careful consideration, but that is not always the case. It is remarkable how many women go overseas without thoroughly analyzing the pros and cons. In this chapter we present some of the motives that send women overseas, offer ideas on how to go about making the decision, discuss alternatives to moving, and present case studies of how some women have made their decisions.

We have grouped women who move overseas into three general categories. The first consists of women who follow their husbands and who are primarily homemakers. The second includes women who follow their husbands and who are homemakers but who also have careers, though the husband is still the primary wage earner. The third is women who move overseas to work in their own professions, either alone or with dependents. This is not a totally new phenomenon. There have always been adventurous women, but competing with men in their roles abroad is relatively recent, and this new status has brought with it new facets to the adjustment process. No matter which category you are in, it is imperative that you examine your motives for moving.

For some it is not a question of *making* a decision to move. Rather it is a requirement of the career that you or your husband chose years before. People in multinational corporations, in the service of government or working for UN or development agencies are obvious examples. Nancy can recall the sense of foreboding she felt when her husband came home with a pledge he had signed to move anywhere in the world for his new employer. There was a list of possible assignments, many of which were far from appealing. The realization that she might some day have to bear her share of making good on that promise made her shudder.

The problem is obvious; what seems like a good idea in the beginning may not seem so good later. You may have a career of your own that you do not want to give up. The children may be at a critical stage in their education or development and you may not want to uproot them. There may be other family issues like aging parents which make moving more difficult than anticipated when the pledge was signed or the original decision made. You may feel a greater need at this point in your life to put roots down rather than pull them up.

Even if it is not your first move overseas, there is still reason to weigh carefully the proposed move. For both of us, and most of our friends, the first decision to move overseas was the easiest. Nancy was so young that no career had been started and "real" as opposed to "student" life would begin overseas. Barbara was at a point where she needed change for continued growth. When these opportunities arose, we were off. However, the decisions to make subsequent moves have been more difficult as family situations and careers have changed.

For Nancy, life became more complicated with the arrival of a child and the development of more serious career considerations. Her husband's motives had not changed. He was born and reared overseas and would happily live in developing countries the rest of his life. Agonizing over each decision, trying to make motives fit the move fell more and more to Nancy. So far his overseas assignments have meshed with her needs so she keeps coming back for more. But each potential move is a time for rethinking rather than automatic agreement.

Recognizing the need to rethink comes from "knowing the territory." Now we know what it means to live out of our own culture. We know, at a gut level, the joys and sorrows we will face as we seek a place for ourselves again. We know the agony of family separation. Unlike making the decision the first time, making it a second time—and again and again—is based on experience.

For Barbara, the first move to another culture was long desired. It was to her husband's country and a sort of homecoming since she knew the culture and loved it. The first move to a distant point came later, when Barbara and her husband needed to add a new dimension to their lives. The second overseas move was inspired by the same ideals. By the third proposed move, Barbara had decided that her chances for doing the sort of work that interested her were too limited overseas. She chose to stay at home most of the time.

There are many different motives for an overseas move. Those listed below are among the most common. However, motives tend to change over time. It is important to reevaluate them with each move. We find, for instance, that many of our friends who started their overseas life with the U.S. Peace Corps or a similar organization grab the next possible opportunity to live overseas because their volunteer experience, though often hard, is remembered as being idyllic. When they return overseas, however, in other types of positions, they are often disappointed. The second tour abroad is much paler by comparison. Women who worked equally with their husbands or on their own find that they are not allowed to work or cannot reach the same level of participation that they remember having before. When the opportunity for another overseas assignment presents itself, they may be less willing to go along or else they have to reexamine their motives; the original ones for working and living overseas are often insufficient for the veteran mover.

MOTIVES

If the possibility of moving abroad was not part of an early career commitment but has developed out of your current employment or constitutes taking a new job, these are the elements most likely to affect your decision:

More money. "We wanted to build a financial reserve and thought a few years abroad would be a small sacrifice for realizing that goal." Financial gain has always been a lure to overseas life. For many it is a perfectly valid reason but does need thorough investigation. It can sustain the breadwinner through all sorts of vicissitudes but it may be insufficient comfort to dependents. Also, with inflation more or less endemic in the world economy, salting away a nest egg may not be so easy. Many people do earn more money living overseas, but expenses are higher than in the past. One may not come out financially ahead. We have known people who have lost money by taking an overseas assignment.

Advancement of spouse's career. "I had a good job but thought that for a while I would not miss it. Besides, the move will be good for my husband's career." Like more money, this motive can bring great satisfaction to the person who advances professionally but little consolation for the one who has left a career behind and realizes, once overseas, that she does miss it.

Getting out of a rut. "We were tired of doing the same jobs and seeing the same people. We were feeling stale and in need of a change." If you are feeling that life has become too predictable and routine, the chance to move overseas may seem like the perfect way to get out of your rut. But remember that the new and exciting can become routine too. This is not to say that you should not take the chance to change your life. For both of us this was a major motivation. But do weigh the decision carefully.

Desire to help those less fortunate. "We jumped at the chance to help people in developing countries and share our knowledge with them." People who have this motivation sometimes, because of their commitment, adjust better than others to some of the rigors of living abroad. But be sure that you are committed, come what may. If you have visions of grateful recipients hanging on your every word and benefiting from all your advice, be prepared for disillusionment. There are many hurdles on the road to technology transfer, and appreciation may not always be the response you get.

Escape from problems. "I thought getting away from my family would relieve the strains between us, but it has just made them worse." Putting distance between yourself and problems at home can be fine at first, but all too soon the problems join you abroad and are often aggravated by that distance. As Harris and Moran point out in their book, *Managing Cultural Differences,* "Problems which are small in the home culture generally become larger overseas. Big family problems in one's native land become disasters in most other countries. Going overseas to start anew is questionable strategy."[1] It is possible that making a complete break can give you a chance to sort yourself out and gain a new perspective. More likely it will highlight and intensify problems. It will depend on you and what your problem is.

Desire for adventure and romance. "We thought that coming overseas would put some romance back into our lives." For many people adventure and romance are the overriding reasons for seeking an overseas position. Unfortunately, both can fade rapidly as the realities of life abroad close in. If this is your motive, be sure it is shared by the entire family and that the challenge of adjusting to new ways of daily living constitutes at least a good portion of the "romance."

---

[1] Philip R. Harris and Robert T. Moran, *Managing Cultural Differences,* 2d ed. (Houston: Gulf Publishing Company, 1987).

FACTORS OF TIMING AND CIRCUMSTANCE

One crucial question is too often ignored: Is this a good *time* to move the family? Wives are pulled from satisfying careers and/or lifestyles with little thought about how they will fare. Children are taken along whether it is the "right time" or not. (More on children in Chapter 9.)

The smoothness of the adjustment process begins with the first step—the decision and how it is made. An example of a decision gone awry involved a group of fifty families who agreed to move to a remote foreign compound to work on a two-year capital development project. Unfortunately, contract negotiations between their company and the local government delayed their departure for more than two years. Suddenly they were called, and all left for the job site without rethinking the decision. They were sobered when we met the wives in an orientation program, trying to come to terms with new babies and school-age children in a place where neither health care nor schools were available. They did manage, but many regretted they had not reconsidered their initial decision.

When a man is transferred, it is normally expected that his wife will be part of the package. She is an asset to the company. If she has entertained for the company at home, maintained social relationships and been the helpmate of her husband's career, she will be expected to perform these duties overseas. Businesses depend on wives to help maintain and build relationships with local people and other foreigners. It is also assumed that a woman will establish a home where serenity reigns and her husband can have the nurturing he needs to perform well. These are expectations with serious ramifications.

For the woman who is primarily a homemaker, there are many considerations. Will she cope in a situation where household help may be available to do the tasks which have always been hers? Will she find her niche in the PTA or other school-related organizations in which her children are involved? Will she enjoy and function well as the wife of Mr. Number One or Two in the office structure and be able to tolerate the pressures that come with that role? Too often, little or no thought is given to what will happen to the dependent wife and homemaker. Her needs and role expectations overseas are not considered. She is cast adrift from her support network with nothing to take its place, no handles to grasp to meet her own needs. She is expected to continue her nurturing role in the family but more often than not finds that she needs nurturing as well. Though she may share her husband's joy in his promotion or new opportunity, her own role is yet to be defined and she is left floundering. If a woman is not prepared to live with this situation and make it work, she should consider putting off the overseas move.

For the wife with a profession, the issues are even more complex. Can she find work in her field? Is she ready to live without her career? Can she find satisfaction in a role designated by her husband's position rather than her own? Will she be able to maintain professional contacts in her own field and even advance in it? After much discussion with many women who have followed their husbands abroad, we have come reluctantly but firmly to the conclusion that the woman who has a serious professional career and is unwilling to give it up or modify her goals significantly should stay at home. We have reached this conclusion mainly because, though there is much interesting work overseas and we have both found it at one time or another, there is little hope of pursuing a career with the concomitant promotions, titles, and job recognition the serious professional needs. The employment of a woman who follows her husband overseas becomes subject to many constraints. Among them are government regulations of the host country or her own country which often prohibit or limit dependent employment (the United States, for instance, maintains cooperative agreements with many countries which disallow the gainful employment of diplomats' wives). There is also the problem—and this is a major one—of constantly starting over again at each new post. A new post may mean a promotion for the primary wage earner of the family, but simply starting from the bottom again for the spouse.

Let us illustrate with our own cases. Nancy is trained in the development field of population management and family planning. In each country she has been to, there have been job opportunities, but it has also been necessary to accept volunteer status, local salaries, short-term consultancies or other modes of temporary employment. Though there has always been a job and, for the most part the jobs have been interesting and timely, they have not allowed her to reach the same level of professional achievement as her husband who is trained and working in the same field. While his career has continued to develop, Nancy has been left to make do with what she can find. For Barbara, a literature graduate, the job opportunities have been considerably fewer. Constant adaptation to the needs of the country of residence has meant accepting jobs which have little or nothing to do with her professional interests.

Problems also arise upon return home. The professional experience needed to reenter the job market may be missing. Potential employers frequently fail to appreciate the significance of work experience overseas. For the professional the decision to move overseas often amounts to deciding whether or not to pursue a career seriously at all.

For the wife who wants to work but not necessarily follow a specific career stream the opportunities are greater. Her paramount asset is flexibility, which enables her to consider a wider range of job opportunities. The willingness to work as a volunteer or at local salary scales will open many doors. Opportunities for work may have to be sought out or created. Thus adaptability, self-confidence, and perseverance are desirable traits to go along with flexibility.

PROFESSIONS WHERE OPPORTUNITIES ARE GREATEST

Perhaps the women with the most adaptable careers are social workers, teachers, anthropologists, secretaries, and artists. Social workers are often able to work even in the smallest expatriate community. There is usually a need for family counselling and help with the special problems of children if the community is willing to use the services of one of its members (trust is sometimes an issue). Often the international school is not prepared to work with children who have special problems and welcomes someone who can provide assistance.

In posts with an international school or schools run by embassies for their nationals, there may be an opportunity to teach. However, unless the teacher has been hired prior to arrival at post, she may face being classed as "local hire" and thus receive fewer "perks" and a lower salary. There are frequently opportunities for teachers of English in the local community as well. For women with this interest, it is a good idea to obtain training in teaching English as a second/foreign language before leaving home, though it is not essential.

Anthropologists can undertake self-directed research or work with other anthropologists on projects in progress. In some places formal permission may be required—and may not be granted.

Good secretaries are usually in demand. Many firms in developing countries are also eager for people who can help their employees improve their English, especially in correspondence and report writing.

For artists, painters, musicians, dramatists, dancers, and writers, the overseas experience can open new creative worlds.

MAKING THE DECISION

How you make the decision to move is crucial. Women are sometimes not consulted until their husbands have received an offer and have more or less come to their own decision. The resentment that follows can play havoc in the couple's relationship. Women who are caught in what seems an inevitable process feel trapped, which causes tension within the family and anger directed toward the country where they will live. The incentive to make a go of it can be weak to nonexistent if a woman feels she is just tagging along (or being dragged along!).

When Nancy asked a group of seminar participants what they saw as the greatest problem facing women overseas, many mentioned this lack of motivation and commitment. Women need to be part of the decision-making process. They need to know what alternatives are available and be able to negotiate what they feel is best for them and for the family as a whole.

Indeed, the decision should be discussed with the entire family. Children need to be included in this process so that they can express their concerns and alert parents to potential problems. It may take a great deal of time and patience, but it is one of our firmest convictions that there should be basic agreement among all those involved in the move. If all can agree on why they are going and jointly commit themselves to make it work, then the problems that arise become much more manageable—and the potential joys much more accessible. If this kind of agreement is not possible, it is important to consider alternatives.

ALTERNATIVE SOLUTIONS

Gone are the days when a family was expected to follow the breadwinner overseas without question. There are now any number of acceptable alternative arrangements to the "lock, stock and barrel" move. Mothers may choose to stay home to avoid interrupting the children's education or to pursue their own careers. In these cases, the father comes home more frequently than otherwise or the dependents travel to see him.

Some companies, especially in the oil industry where work locations are remote, have been experimenting with new overseas assignment patterns. Some rotate men to the field for three months and then home for one. The family never moves. Some move families to the capital city of the country and schedule employees to the field for one- or two-week assignments. It is increasingly rare for a company to force the family to live in a remote complex while the husband builds a road or digs a well, though it still happens.

Alternative lifestyles are no longer rare among "expat" families. An example is Barbara's village in England in which six women live a "semi-bachelor" existence, following their own paths while their husbands work overseas. It may not be an ideal life but it is possible.

Do not be afraid to consider the alternatives. The more women require employing organizations to consider family needs, the more responsive these organizations will become.

CASES IN POINT

How have some women balanced their own needs against the desire to keep the family together? How have others managed by making the decision not to go? Here are cases of women we have known from Cairo to Kathmandu, Sao Paulo to Sydney.

Deborah

Deborah is a clinical nurse first and a homemaker second. Her first overseas experience was with her husband in voluntary service. They lived in a village where she managed the local health clinic. She was immersed and committed. Following this service, Deborah's husband was employed by a large development organization. Conflict arose over the organization's regulations against dependent employment, but Deborah got around the regulations and continued to work.

When her husband was transferred to another country, Deborah was prohibited by local regulations from working as a clinical nurse, though there was a desperate need for health care personnel. This was hard for her to accept. When she looked around, she found that other women in the medical field faced the same problem. She chose to organize these women and spearheaded the development of a professional organization for medically trained women to provide continuing education and private medical counselling services to the expatriate community and to schedule regular meetings of professionals for mutual support. The organization has grown and has had a positive impact; it has provided assistance to the expatriate community in the development of a health management project and conducted infant feeding practice workshops throughout the country. A major business in the community also hired her to develop a health handbook for its workers.

In spite of this apparent success, she will not go back. At the age of thirty-six, she decided that she has to live where she can do the job she loves and receive professional recognition for it. She left this parting note:

> Heck, I don't really know *what* I'd do if I were staying! I'm just glad I'm not. As the situation stands, I feel any more time and effort spent here would be spinning wheels. Sure, there is *always* something different, something to learn. But I'm tired of *searching* all the time and then, if I am *allowed* to proceed, I'd like to be recognized. My resume looks great—but who cares?

Ruth

Ruth chose not to follow. As a successful career woman in her mid-forties, she had carved a niche for herself in her home area. She did not want to leave. Though her children were independent, she felt they needed the continuity of home. Her husband travels home frequently to be with the family. She and each of the children have made trips to see him. It has been a workable solution to the problem of maintaining individual integrity in the family.

Laura

Laura is an accountant. She agreed with her family to one tour overseas, where they would live in a large city. Laura went to her employer and through his contacts compiled a list of companies involved in joint ventures with U.S. counterparts which might be able to use her services. When she arrived, she settled her child in school and interviewed with several of the companies, quickly finding a job which fit her needs and interests. She worked for eighteen months before she left the job to travel and to work on a business idea of her own. Soon thereafter she opened in her home a private accounting service for expatriates. She thus could pursue her career while having the flexibility she needed to travel and learn more about the country. She has since repatriated and has used the experience gained overseas to establish a similar business in her home town.

Louise

Louise is a lawyer who worked for a government agency in her home country. Her husband, who worked for a development agency, long resisted being posted overseas because of the negative effect on his wife's career. They had come to the point, however, when both felt that the time to move overseas had arrived. Their child was a pre-teen so they were still flexible about her schooling. If the husband had not taken the offered overseas assignment, it would have negatively affected his career. Louise was at a point in her own career where she could afford to take a two-year leave of absence. Before leaving, they agreed that she would stay in the post for only two years, returning home with their daughter at that time, while her husband might stay on for as long as an additional two years before returning himself.

There are many examples of women who, in the past, have followed their husbands from post to post with (supposedly) not so much as a murmur of protest. We find that such women are fewer these days. Most of the women we know decide to move or not on a case-by-case or country-by-country basis. We do not doubt that this is best. It is impossible to say that what was right when we were twenty-five will still be right when we are thirty-five and again at forty-five or fifty.

Nancy's in-laws were missionaries in a large Asian country. When they accepted the overseas assignment, they agreed with the mission board that they would spend their entire working life in that one place. They left their home country in 1940 with the agreement that they would have their first leave after five years. The war intervened, and they were unable to depart until seven years later with their two "babies" (one six, the other nearly two) who had been born in the intervening years. They returned to their overseas post for another seven years, had a one-year break and went back again until 1960, when they finally left because of health and career reasons. Few missionaries make this kind of commitment any more. It seems unrealistic for all but the most dedicated.

Because even a two-year period can seem like an eternity to a family which has moved overseas for the wrong reason or which has not carefully explored their individual motives for coming, we urge you to ponder your decision. If you decide to uproot yourself and your family, be sure you know what you are doing and why.

three

Preparation for Departure

Most women we know who have moved overseas feel they did not have enough time to prepare. One family we know is on their first overseas assignment. They were given a weekend to decide whether they wanted to move ten thousand miles from home with four children under the age of eight. They said yes and all kinds of support was promised. Yet the woman received only one piece of information, "You'll love it! It's fun to live there." This kind of information from a company that does 90 percent of its business overseas! After six months of settling in, she does love it, thanks to the marshaling of her own resources and the support of friends she found. Then there is the experience of a woman whose husband works for a company with ten years' experience in the country to which they were being sent. She was told in her briefing that *nothing* was available, and she purchased, at no small expense, commodities and food for a two-year period. She arrived, and on her first trip to a supermarket found all the goods she had just purchased and brought with her stocked to the ceiling. The prices were lower too.

Whether they did or did not have enough time or the right information matters less than how they felt. What tends to happen is that women get caught in the physical preparations that have to be made, sorting the household goods, arranging for packing and storage, and planning the trip. Little time is left for or allocated to mental and emotional preparation, learning the language, doing some substantial background reading, or getting ready for a change in lifestyle.

But there is more. Maryanne Vandervelde, in her perceptive book *The Changing Role of the Corporate Wife,* spoke of the stresses experienced by the wives of mobile business executives:

> Moving in and of itself is not bad. In fact, many women experience excitement in the change and are able to see moving in terms of new opportunities. But the stress involved should not be minimized. One cannot move without having to adapt in many ways, and moving presents tremendous challenges to one's identity.
>
> Although it is reasonable to think of moving in terms of opportunities, one cannot deny that there are losses. The losses for skilled and professional women may be significant as they search in vain for similar or equal positions, but the losses for the housewife with small children are also painful. Men too experience losses in a move, but the executive is usually welcomed into the new community through his work, and he almost always makes the move with more feeling of purpose. A man who works does not quickly develop friends, but he immediately has a circle of acquaintances with at least their work in common. Any woman who does not work will probably find it much more difficult to develop relationships.[1]

Vandervelde's corporate wives are moving only within their own culture and even then the strains are acute. How much more stress you need to be prepared for when leaving your own culture to travel the world!

We'll examine here the issues involved in both emotional and physical preparation.

---

[1] Maryanne Vandervelde, *The Changing Role of the Corporate Wife* (New York: Mecox Publishing Company, 1979).

EMOTIONAL PREPARATION

Much is needed in the way of *emotional preparation*. Major upheaval is about to occur! We will go into the subject of emotional adjustment more thoroughly in Chapter 6. It is useful, however, to consider adjustment issues at the outset as part of the preparation process. Here, briefly stated, are the principal factors most commonly associated with overseas adjustment.

1. Everything will be new. There will be little to provide you with a sense of comfortable familiarity.

2. You may be in your own critical life passage, adjusting to a new family situation which consumes emotional energy and limits the ability to adjust to other new factors in your life.

3. Your personal identity may get lost in the transition from Chicago or Glasgow to Lagos or Tokyo.

4. Privacy could become a thing of the past if you hire a houseful of servants.

5. You are not a pioneer so you will have to live with the images and stereotypes others have implanted in the minds of your hosts.

6. In some locations sojourners become part of a minority group, with all that implies.

7. The status of women in your host country will affect your mobility, your opportunities for interpersonal relations and, in some cases, virtually your total lifestyle.

8. Loneliness can be a constant companion in the early months.

9. Learning about a new culture takes constant effort, yet you will still often do the "wrong" thing and feel out of place.

10. Everyday living patterns will change as working hours may be longer than at home.
11. After a time you begin to feel out of touch with what's new at home.
12. An excess of time on your hands can be your friend or enemy.
13. The possibility of crime and violence subjects you to real and/or imagined dangers.
14. Self-confidence can easily be eroded as you become aware of the magnitude of the changes you are undergoing in some areas of your life.
15. You will be called upon to fulfill your nurturing role when you may need nurturing yourself.
16. If you are in a biracial marriage, you may find yourself among people who disapprove.

In the hectic predeparture days, setting aside time to give these issues some thought will be time well spent. We suggest some coping strategies in Chapter 6.

PHYSICAL PREPARATION

What to Do First

Seek information about your new home. The most obvious place to inquire is the embassy or consulate of the country to which you are going. Depending on the country, this may or may not prove useful. Many countries in Asia, the Middle East and Latin America do not provide much in the way of practical information through their embassies abroad. There is information for tourists, but not much in the way of help for those who are planning an extended stay. However, it is worth a try. You may be lucky, especially if you can go in person and speak to the Information Officer or other senior official. Some of the larger embassies have libraries which you may be able to use. If the embassy or consulate is too far away, a telephone call may bring results.

Move on to your local library. Most librarians enjoy a challenge and should be able to unearth a relevant book or information source even for a small country.

Your sending organization may have provided you with a post report or briefing document. It will usually cover such things as population, geography, climate, trade policies, etc. It should also include practical details of what to take with you. We recommend that you use shipping instructions as a guideline only, not as a bible to be followed to the letter. You can be misled, as Barbara was when her post report suggested taking large quantities of elastic. She took yards of it, and used twelve inches in two years!

If you receive no information from your organization, ask for it. If there appears to be no mechanism for providing it, you may want to raise the issue. Excellent materials on living abroad have been developed by women who were provided no advance information and did not want others to have the same experience.

Try to get the names of one or two people who live in your assigned country to whom you can write with questions, or try to find people who have recently returned from it. Most people are eager to share their overseas experiences with others. Organizations may help. In Britain, information can be gleaned from the Women's Corona Society,[2] formed by Foreign Office wives but open to any woman living overseas. Although you should take the comments of "old hands" with a grain of salt until you can form your own opinions, the practical information they give can be valuable.

The foreign student advisor at a nearby college or university may be able to suggest ways to gather information, and

---

[2] Women's Corona Society, Commonwealth House, 18 Northumberland Avenue, London WC2N 5BJ, England; tel: 71-839-7908.

your or your husband's employer might be able to introduce you to expatriates from the country.

Styles of Dress

We both feel that how one dresses is important while living overseas and has a significant effect on our hosts and on our relationships with them. In some countries, there are strict codes. For example:

A Malawi Tourist Board brochure reads: "Women must wear dresses which cover their knees while standing up. Men will not be allowed into the country with long hair or bell-bottom trousers."

From a brochure at the Intercontinental Hotel in Riyadh, Saudi Arabia: "Women shall wear long dresses with long sleeves. Men shall not wear open shirts, tight trousers or chains."

Most countries are not so strict, but they do have customs in dress which, if you follow them, will make you feel more comfortable. A sensitivity to local dress customs will also please your hosts.

This all goes for men too. No shorts are worn at work, for instance, in countries like Indonesia and Saudi Arabia even on scorching days.

You are seen before you speak. No matter how polite you are, if your dress offends you will not be heard.

Children and Schools

If you have children and want to enroll them in school, now is the time to inquire. Schools overseas usually have quotas for each year, based on facilities and the number of teachers, and it is wise to get your children's names on the list as promptly as you can. You may want to enroll them in an international school. In larger posts, however, you will often find you have a choice of a specific nationality school or an international school. In Jakarta, for instance, there are schools run by the British, French, Japanese, Dutch and Germans, as well as a large international school which is American in orientation. Whatever you decide, write as soon as possible to get the address of the school and make contact with the principal or headmaster. If your organization cannot provide you with names and addresses of schools, write to your embassy in the country and ask them to supply you with the information. The schools are only too happy to send a prospectus and application forms since they want to know in advance about new students. You can always change your mind on arrival. The International Schools Service[3] publishes a directory of overseas schools and provides other services which may be of help to you.

Accommodation on Arrival

Housing is covered in Chapter 4 but for immediate accommodation on arrival we advocate the use of a "leave" house (the house of someone who will be on vacation when you arrive). This is usually more satisfactory than staying in a hotel and can ease the transition to your new country. You will get used to having household help who are trained, and you will discover what to look for when searching for your own house regarding such matters as electric supply, water, location, etc. It can be a more comfortable setting than a hotel, especially if you have children. Your organization should know of people who will be on leave when you arrive. You can contact the family directly or work through friends in the country. Perfect strangers are often willing to sublet their houses because they prefer to have someone living in them while they are away. They advertise within the company or in organizational newsletters for "house-sitters." Pursue this early and you may be lucky. If you cannot find such a house before you go, try to do so when you arrive. Check with office personnel and notice boards and inquire at the local expat

---

[3] International Schools Service, P.O. Box 5910, Princeton, NJ, 08543 U.S.A.

church and international women's organizations. It may save you a couple of months in a hotel. If you cannot find a house to "sit," try to locate an apartment on a short-term basis or a residence hotel which offers kitchen facilities—no matter how minimal.

Costs of Moving and Settling In

Get as much information as you can on the expenses you will incur while settling into your new home. These can be very high in some countries, especially those where you have to pay a large advance on your rent or even several years' rent in a lump sum. If you will be responsible for finding and paying for your housing, you should try to get a clear idea of what expenses to expect and plan accordingly. Some organizations provide loans to their employees to cover immediate expenses. If you are planning to buy new furniture after you arrive in lieu of shipping your own, you will have to make down payments when orders are placed. You may also have to pay to have your goods shipped from the port of entry to your home. Some ready cash will be needed.

Predeparture Concerns of the Working Woman

If you wish to find a job in your assigned country, you should attempt to make plans prior to departure. Obtain a list of contacts through your organization and write to prospective employers, enclosing your resume. Also ask about labor laws and other constraints on the employment of dependents.

A good source of information is women who are already in the country. Identify some likely people and write prior to departure, describing your skills and what you would like to do. This gives them a chance to begin looking on your behalf. They are normally happy to do so. Alternatively, contacts can sometimes be found through the embassy of your assigned country. It is important to remember, however, that in some countries employment information is virtually impossible to obtain until you are there.

Predeparture Medical Check

Make sure your body is in good "working order" before embarking for your new home. A physical examination for each family member is highly recommended, as is a dental check. Take care of any problems before moving. If you wear glasses, have an eye examination and carry a second pair of glasses *and* a copy of your prescription with you. If you wear contact lenses, you will want to check with your doctor about their continued use if the air at your destination is dusty or contains high pollution levels. Many people find that they are unable to wear them while abroad.

Ask your doctor for a copy of your medical records. Check on the availability of any prescription medicines you need and, unless you can definitely obtain them at your destination, take an extra supply (also get their generic names). If you do take medication with you, you will need a letter from your doctor describing the medicine and its use; this is required by customs in a number of countries, Saudi Arabia, for example. If you can rely on the postal service, you may want to set up a system with your doctor or pharmacist to send medication as needed.

Travel and Shipping Arrangements

Travel and shipping can be nightmares for the uninitiated, though they do not have to be. Armed with good information, the old-timer takes them in stride, and even for the first-timer they can be less intimidating than anticipated. Most important is to obtain clear instructions from your organization on procedures and allowances. *Do not depend on hearsay or the experience of others.* Go directly to the administrative officer in charge and write all the instructions down if the information is not already in printed form.

Each organization differs in what it will allow. Some give air freight shipments, others only sea freight, and still others allow a combination. Some let you use the military postal service for immediate needs. For travel, some organizations require that you use a national airline; others do not care what airline is used, just so you arrive by the most direct route. A few organizations allow business or first class for trips over a certain number of hours or for people over a certain height.

If you get an air freight allowance, we strongly recommend sending some things by air, even though it means additional sorting. Air freight will normally be safer from water, pest, or pilferage damage. Send by air those things you value highly or know you will need immediately. Air freight should be fast (though there are some countries where customs clearance of air shipments takes much longer than that for sea freight, so it pays to check). Send things that you need immediately or which will make your life easier from the day of arrival, such as a small cassette player and some tapes, pictures and picture wire, children's favorite toys and books, table and bed/bath linen, herbs for cooking, kitchen utensils, and a few basic tools. The period when you first arrive can be the most difficult. Anything you can take to make your accommodations feel more like home will be appreciated by the family. Barbara once spent two months in a leave house without any music because the house did not have audio equipment and she felt quite deprived!

Most organizations require that you get two or three estimates from different companies for the shipping of household goods. If this is so, start early, as the bids will have to be submitted to the organization for approval. Use reliable, established firms with experience in overseas shipping, especially if you are sending goods by sea. Packing overseas shipments requires expertise which is quite different from that needed to move goods domestically. Find out how much insurance coverage is provided and what it includes. You may want to purchase additional insurance to cover such things as pianos, art work, silverware, stamp collections, or other items whose value may exceed the allowed coverage or which may be specifically excluded under the organization's policy. Because of insurance "rules," let the packers do the work; you supervise.

If it is necessary to store household goods, the same

advice applies. Start early and find a reliable firm which is experienced in storage. More horror stories come from this aspect of living overseas than almost any other. Fly-by-night operations can go bankrupt while you are away. We speak from bitter experience. Barbara arrived back in England after three years overseas to find her furniture about to be auctioned by liquidators to pay the storage company's bankruptcy debts. The furniture was recovered but it was in poor condition and she had to pay exorbitant bills to get it out of storage. The insurance coverage with the firm was worthless.

Many organizations pay for storage of household goods, particularly if furniture is provided in your assigned country by your employer. Check on this and on how payment of storage bills is to be handled.

One of the hard facts of a mobile life is that things you value can get damaged or stolen. People who move often acquire an admirable "easy come, easy go" attitude toward material possessions. To prevent grief, we advocate that you do not send anything abroad which you really treasure. Your goods can be insured but many things are irreplaceable. It is best to store them. This applies especially to antique furniture, valuable books, family photographs, paintings, or family archives. Even the best shipping firm cannot guarantee that your goods will not mildew or be ruined by water while sitting at port in a tropical climate.

Shipping the Car

This can be a difficult issue. You will obviously need some means of getting around in your host country. If the employed member of the family is to be provided with a vehicle, you may still want a personal car. Check to see if the "office" car can be used by the family for after-hours and week-end transportation. If a driver is to be provided, it may be possible to use him and the vehicle for domestic needs when they are not being used for business.

If this option is not open to you and you will need a

personal car, find out about shipping regulations. Some countries do not allow the importation of vehicles; in Indonesia, for example, you are obliged to buy a locally assembled car.

If the country you are going to does permit the importation of cars, you will need to arrange for both shipping and receipt or delivery on the other end. Your organization should be able to give you details.

Sailings of ships that transport cars to your assigned country can be few and far between. Scheduling can be trying. You will want the car soon after you arrive, so you may have to send it weeks or even months before you go yourself.

Remember that servicing and availability of parts may be a problem, especially with exotic makes and models. Consider shipping a supply of parts. Cars using unleaded fuel will also be a problem in developing countries since unleaded fuel is generally not available. The most basic "work-horse" kind of vehicle is the best for overseas living. Reliability is particularly important, coupled with sturdiness and a size suitable for narrow, congested streets. In the end, you may want to purchase your car locally, which you can often do from another expat whose assignment is at or near completion.

Pets

If you are planning to ship pets, inquire about the regulations early. Most airlines can ship animals, but it can be a traumatic time for the pets. You can lessen the trauma by trying to schedule them on flights which avoid their having to wait on the ground for extended periods. The best arrangement is to have a trusted person at home send the pets after you have arrived in your assigned country. Then you can meet them. There are kennels which can handle these arrangements. Special inoculations may be required. Usually a certificate of rabies vaccination is sufficient, but do check. Quarantine regulations can be strict. Great Britain requires that any animal brought into the country be quarantined for six months. Australia allows no animals at all. In most Moslem countries dogs are considered unclean and, although not prohibited, may create problems with servants and neighbors.

Pets can create problems for the mobile family, and you would be wise to consider leaving them behind, though weigh carefully the role of the pet in your family before making that decision. Pets can usually be found locally to fill the gap if you do leave yours behind.

MAKING THE JOURNEY

Traveling together to a new country can be exciting, or it can be a time of racing to meet deadlines and arriving upset and tired. Naturally we suggest you strive for the former. Even if you have to be in your assigned country in a hurry, try to carve out a few days to see something along the way and spend some quiet time together. Normally the days before departure are filled with tension. Tears and laughter follow one behind the other. Take some time to relax and breathe deeply before facing all the new things that lie ahead.

We recommend that the family travel as a unit, rather than the father going ahead. The trip out does not need to include major sightseeing adventures which have you running from bus to attraction and back again. Instead, stop off in a place where the main attraction is an atmosphere congenial to relaxation. For Nancy that choice was, and continues to be, a quiet stretch of beach in Hawaii. Each family member looks forward to the lazy day on the beach (they do it even when they have only twenty-four hours to spare). The break in Ha erwaii is refreshing and brings the family closer together.

Travel by air is fun for the well-prepared family. Try to arrange seating when you make your reservations, and remember to order special foods, if required, in advance.

Plan carefully what to carry by hand. Here are some items you will want to include:

1. Passports and all other important *documents,* including copies of marriage licenses and birth certificates

(originals should be stored at home), as well as health records and papers you will need on arrival.

2. *Traveler's checks* for the adult members of the family in their own names.

3. *Identification tags* for the children, either pinned on shirts if they are young or on a travel bag if they are old enough to be responsible for their things.

4. The favorite *snugly toy* or *blanket* for young children. It is comforting to know that a stuffed animal from home is coming along for the ride. Also some *books*.

5. Any *medication* you think might be needed, including aspirin or a substitute, antacid tablets, and a decongestant.

6. An extra set of children's *clothes* and *pajamas* for a night flight and *toothbrushes* and *toothpaste* on very long flights.

7. A few *surprises*. Delays are easier to live through and new surroundings do not seem so forbidding when there is plenty of amusement.

8. Extra *snack food*. Chewing raisins or sugarless gum is excellent for clearing the ears on takeoff and landing.

If you are ready for the trip, you can be relaxed and enjoy it, and the children will be happy and excited. Children reflect the attitudes and tensions of their parents, so the more relaxed you are, the more comfortable they will be both during the trip and on arrival.

four

—

Settling In

You have arrived! The details of settling in may not be fore-most in your mind as you disembark, but you will soon be confronted with the task. We hope that you will quickly find an ample number of friends and others who can help in the process. In the meantime, we offer here practical guidelines for finding a house and furniture, enrolling children in school and arranging other activities for them, learning the language, finding friends and living with new ways of doing things.

PRACTICAL DETAILS

Housing the Family

Housing heads the "settling in" list. Start looking as soon as you arrive. Remember the "leave" house suggestion for the interim period before your own home is found and furnished.

What do you need to look for in a house? There are several considerations.

Number of Rooms. What are the needs of your family? Do the children need separate rooms? Do you need an office? Will you require entertainment space? Will you have live-in help? Do you need a garden?

Location. Must you be near the school or is it more important to be near places of work? Do you want to be within walking distance of the markets and shopping areas? Do you want to live near other foreigners or would you rather be in a neighborhood of host country nationals? Will you have your own transportation or rely on public transport? Are your children old enough to go out on their own via public transport or will they rely on you?

Utilities. What are your electricity needs? How many air conditioners/heaters or other appliances do you plan to have? What is the voltage (110 in the U.S.A., 220/240 in most other countries), current (AC or DC), and wattage (total amount of electrical current needed to run all appliances and lighting)? What about water supply? Is there a pump (if water has to be pumped to a holding tank) or city water? Is there a backup system? Do some areas have better public utilities than others? If you will be living in an apartment building, is there an elevator, and if so, how dependable is it? Are there frequent power failures? If so, lower floors are best.

General Ambience. What about noise? Schools, markets, shopping centers, and mosques are all noisy neighbors. How much traffic is there on the street?

Rank your questions in order of importance to you. Try to work through the housing office of your organization if there is one. If not, you may have to rely on word of mouth from new acquaintances. In many large cities, there are helpful real estate agents who deal in rental housing. However, sometimes they are not reliable, so be on your guard. Be prepared to compromise. You may not find your dream home but you can find something comfortable.

When you have found the house, seek assistance either from your organization or a qualified local lawyer or notary for the rental contract. Rentals can be complex. In Jakarta, for example, a contract is drawn up through a local lawyer who specializes in the field. If your organization has a legal office, have the contract checked there. Be aware that in many cities all rent must be paid in advance for the duration of the contract. This can amount to a very large sum, and you must have the cash when the contract is signed. Even in places where all the rent is not paid in advance, a fairly large advance can be required.

It is often necessary to have repairs and redecorating done before you can move in. If possible, insist that the work be completed before you pay any rent, or you might compromise by paying a small amount toward the rent that can be used to cover the cost of materials. If you pay and move in, there is a greater chance the work will not be completed or will drag on, much to your discomfort. In either case, keep close watch on the progress to make sure things are done to your satisfaction.

Document the condition of the house or apartment during a "walk-through" with the owner or agent. You might be held responsible when you leave for preexisting damages unless they are noted.

Furnishing Your House

You can now enjoy the search for furnishings. If you are shipping most of your furniture, you will be looking only for accessories. If you have not shipped them you will have a wider scope for the pleasures of shopping. In tropical countries the local rattan furniture is suitable for the climate, attractive and not too expensive. Many houses are beautifully furnished with rattan and curtains of the local fabric (Thai cottons, southeast Asian batiks, or even jute.). If you prefer Western-style furniture, you can probably get anything you want copied if you have a picture. Barbara furnished an apartment in New Delhi with upholstered furniture which made the transition back to the West with great aplomb. Study the fabrics. There are many choices and the prices are often less than back home. Even raw silk seats on your dining room chairs are economically viable in some places.

Rely on people who are settled to advise you on shopping places and prices. Most shopkeepers in the Middle East and Asia will bargain, but you need to know the going rates before you can bargain properly, so ask around. Try not to become discouraged by delays. Remember that your Western sense of time may not be shared by your hosts. Delivery dates may be merely a "best estimate" or an attempt to please you when you look undone.

Plan on taking three to six months to get settled. From this perspective the mishaps and delays you experience will be less frustrating. A family can rarely be settled before three months; six months is common. There are many things to be done and they cannot all be accomplished in the first week. Sea shipments may arrive in three months, take a month to clear customs, and then another month to get in order. Relax through the settling-in process; take it one day at a time.

Some organizations provide their employees with "survival kits" consisting of household essentials (linens, crockery and cutlery, small appliances, etc.). If yours does not, local expatriate women's organizations may. Both the United Nations Women's Association and the American Women's Association provide such kits in some places. They can make the initial weeks in your new home much more comfortable.

School and Activities for the Children

Settle the children as quickly as possible. Go to school with them for registration and orientation. Talk with administrative personnel and try to meet the teacher and others who will be working with your child. Inquire about school activities and enroll your children in those of interest. Help them find their classrooms and explore other parts of the school together. Knowing the way around will boost a child's confidence on the first day of school. Most schools are open a week prior to the start of the school year, so it should not be hard to establish contact.

Find other families that have children the same age as yours and introduce your children to them before the start of school. Just seeing a familiar face will help your child on the first day. You also may want to come along that first day and stay until your child feels comfortable—and one day may not be enough. Patience is the key. When we think how much is new for the children, it is not surprising that they might want to hang on a bit tightly for a few days.

When you live overseas it is necessary to manage the lives of your children, whatever their ages, more actively than you do at home. In a typical neighborhood at home, your child can peddle off on a bicycle and come home an hour later for milk and cookies with a new friend. This will not be possible in most foreign countries. You need to seek out friends and activities for your children. They may be available through organizations or clubs or they may be centered in the school, but sports, music, drama, dance, and local cultural activities are almost always available.

In some places community organizations have been developed just to cater to the interests of children. Alas, in other locations they have not. Here a newcomer must be an activist. One family had an interest in computers and invited others to join the children as they programmed their home computer. Soon there was an active computer club meeting in their home. They gained a wide circle of friends as a result. Another example is a soccer program developed for children of all ages by parents who coached and refereed the games. Scouting is a popular activity in many countries. In all of these, interest is as important as expertise. The children benefit from our enthusiastic support and involvement.

Your preschool child may need a school or playgroup. Most of the good preschools overseas are run by women who were interested in finding some form of organized play for their children. One of the largest and most attractive preschools we have known was started by just such a woman. It became a training center for host country teachers.

Consider also what can be done to make your new country *home* to your children. They will be feeling the effects of the move and will need guidance to adjust smoothly. Further discussion of children can be found in Chapter 9.

Language Learning

If you want to learn the language—and you should—but did not have time before departure, now is the time to start.

There are a variety of ways to learn a language. We offer the following as suggestions, leaving you to decide which method fits your time and your capabilities. If you are adept at learning languages, we envy you. If you are a little slow, you have plenty of company. But be assured, based on our own experience, it can still be done, and your life overseas will be far richer. Most important, do not put it off; start as soon as you arrive.

1. Take an intensive course. This is the best method if one is available and you have the time. Some organizations provide a course for employees and dependents. The format varies, with classes meeting each morning or all day for a period of a week up to a month. This provides an excellent base for continuation on your own and enough basic vocabulary to help you immediately in everyday communication.

2. Private tutoring. You will have greater flexibility if you can arrange for private tutoring at your home or office. There are two disadvantages to this method, however. You may not be able to find a skilled tutor, and you may not be self-motivated enough to study. Progress can be slow. However, if you must use a tutor, find one through other expatriates. If you cannot leave the house in the early stages of your stay, it may be the only way to obtain formal instruction. We have both used tutors and found them valuable, though we always combined the tutoring with long stays in rural areas where little or no English was spoken.

3. Learn from books and tapes. Some people can learn languages through self-instructional methods, others

cannot. Motivation is particularly important here, as is a good ear. But it is difficult to develop language-speaking skills through self-instruction. If the other two options are not open to you, however, this method is worth a try.

In order to really learn a language, you have to use it. This is nothing new, but it bears repeating since we find that people are often reluctant to use the language abilities they possessed as children. It is natural to feel embarrassed when you try to say something and realize by the blank stares that you are not communicating. You go back to feeling like a child again, when you repeated the simplest phrases while trying to find the right way to say what you meant. Yet we must seek out opportunities to use the language. Start in your own home, with the household help. In some places there are conversation groups which bring expatriates together with women of the host country for a morning of coffee and talk. Sometimes the conversation is combined with lessons in the local cuisine or with learning handicrafts. The market is another place to work on vocabulary and learn new words. The bargaining process, age-old and important in many countries, affords a perfect opportunity to speak the local language using simple phrases— and you return home triumphantly with your purchase.

Set aside a specific time of the day to study language. The rewards of communicating well will be worth the tedium of vocabulary memorization and grammar study, but don't get bogged down in rules. It is most important to begin to speak—even if your tenses are mixed up.

Small children seem to learn a new language with little effort. Schools generally require study of the local language and preschoolers pick it up from the maid or on the playground. If language learning is important to you, your children should know it and be encouraged to learn in a formal setting. Some families try speaking the local language at meals or other desig-nated times so they can practice. Beware the bruised ego when your children speak with more fluency than you do.

Unrealistic Expectations

Most of us look forward to our new life with great antici-pation. We build a picture in our minds based on whatever information is available, which too often consists of guide-book descriptions, stories from people who vacationed there, and materials from historical or literary works which capture the drama of the society more than its day-to-day reality. To this we add our own wishful thinking, filling in where hard information is lacking.

Unfortunately, our new home usually fails to live up to our expectations. What seemed exotic and exciting in guide-books is hot, dirty or noisy. The tropical paradise or cosmo-politan city loses some of its appeal when we are struggling to settle in.

Prior to her first move to Indonesia, Nancy had been shown guidebooks of the tropical island of Bali. Before depart-ing, she dreamed of a house on the beach, coral reefs to ex-plore, a swim or sail at the end of a hard day. The dream was reinforced by a side trip to the Philippines (on the way to Indonesia), where the friends they visited had a beach and reef right out of the dream itself. After several idyllic days on the Philippine beach, she arrived in Jakarta. What a shock to find, not Bali, but a teeming city full of automobiles, pedicabs, and people. The nearest beach was three hours by car on a road meant only for the fearless. Eventually she found her Indone-sian "tropical paradise," but it was not in Jakarta!

Some women have quite the opposite experience. One was told by relatives who had visited the city where she was going to live that it was the worst place they had ever been. When she arrived she was delighted to find tree-lined subur-ban streets and lovely homes with running water and electric-ity. But how much better it is to be able to say: "It is not as bad as I thought it would be," rather than suffer disappoint-ment.

Networking or Finding Your Support Group

Any discussion of adjusting to life overseas should emphasize the need to find people with whom we can communicate easily and on whom we can call in times of stress. In short, we need a network of supportive, compatible people. But finding them is not as easy as it sounds. In the first place, we may not be ready to jump into new relationships when we are keenly aware of how painful it was to depart from old friends. Getting close to someone means that someday we will have to part and go through all that emotional upheaval again. When we said those last good-byes at the airport, we were not thinking of our motives for going overseas or the dreams we had. We were thinking of all the good things and people we were leaving behind. It takes time to get over this feeling and face forming new relationships.

We have a friend who puts it this way:

> I have never been good at saying good-bye. But I do it because I know that I have to go through it. I would never be able to live with myself if I did not take the time to say good-bye to my parents or a good friend and then something happened to them before I could get back home. Yet after I say all those emotional farewells, a part of me closes down. I can't face, for a while, saying bright and cheery "hellos" all over the place. I find myself retreating from it for a time because the pain of knowing that I will have to say "goodbye" to that person is more than I can stand at first. I find, though, that I don't stay in retreat too long and it is always worth it to get out there and meet those new people and find the ones who will be my friends. I have learned after many years overseas that these people, so sadly left, turn up over and over again. That's what gets me through both the "hellos" and the "good-byes."

During the first few weeks many people will welcome you. All of them are potential friends, but how do you sort them out? Slowly, it is suggested. The problem, however, is that your time of greatest need for help in problem solving and sharing concerns is when you first arrive. You cannot dump it all on your family at a time when they are turning to you for strength. It is also very important to distinguish between those who will be friends and those for whom your problems will be grist for the gossip mill.

This gossip mill, present wherever one lives, is often more active, potent, and insidious overseas, partly because expatriate communities are small and generally close-knit and partly because too many people have too much time on their hands. Gossip is ugly no matter where it occurs, but in a strange land, when one is new and not sure of the truth of things, it can distort reality and be extremely hurtful. It can also lead you seriously astray as you develop attitudes toward your host country. Gossip mongers tend to be malcontents who blame all their own problems on their hosts.

How do you go about making fruitful contacts? First of all, try to keep your priorities straight and keep in mind the goals you have set for yourself. Perhaps the first step is to find others with similar interests. If you are a tennis player, find the tennis clubs (most overseas posts have at least one and usually several, and prices are normally cheaper than at home). If you are a bridge player, ask around to find the "best game in town." And so on. Just by asking, your interests and skills will become known and you will be sought out to join in. If you find your first experience is not to your liking, you need not go again.

Children's activities afford opportunities to find friends, not only for the children. One woman met her first friends through her son's soccer and her daughter's scouting programs.

Some women forget that in order to meet the kinds of people they would like to know, they have to go where those people congregate. If you do not intend to spend your time playing poolside bridge at the American Club, that is not the place to find women who share your interests.

Many have said to us, "I'm not a joiner so I don't intend to go to the women's association meetings. I don't have time for coffee mornings and gossip." We sympathize with those feelings but feel that newcomers should attend *some* club functions in order to find out what they are like and make sure they do not miss enjoyable people or interesting activities. These meetings are a time to see and be seen, to let people know who you are and find out about the organization and the women who are involved in it. The focus of these groups varies from place to place. In some countries women's organizations are very active in welfare and cultural programs. In others, they are strictly social. The one in your new country should not be judged by stereotypes or by those you have encountered before. In one country, Barbara became active in a women's group and worked on a monthly bulletin which expanded over time and gave a number of people a much wider scope for their research and writing. Women in these organizations are often quite knowledgeable about local crafts, shopping, and travel. So we suggest you go, listen, and ask questions. Reserve decisions about making further commitments until you are settled.

In some countries an American Women's Association or its equivalent will have an office, staffed by long-term residents, which maintains an information bank. Whether you are American or not, this is a place to ask questions. Some embassies and companies have an office for family assistance (called the Community Liaison Office in American embassies and large consulates general). This office too is usually managed by an experienced resident and can provide useful information. Use it well if you have one.

Many women are accustomed to being self-sufficient in most things and like to "go it alone." They may find asking for help difficult, fearing it may be perceived as a sign of weakness. Yet asking for help is an essential survival skill in an overseas setting. There are usually lots of people who are willing to be of assistance (they know what you are experiencing), but they will not know what is needed unless you ask.

Health Support

Managing an illness in the family is difficult during the best of times and produces great tension when the family is not prepared. The family's medical records should be carried with you and filed in a convenient location. Some organizations have clinics staffed with expatriate medical personnel. If yours does not, you will have to explore the medical services used by the expatriate community. Both a physician for the adult family members and a pediatrician for the children should be identified and visited before an illness occurs. Keep a book or file of emergency numbers near the telephone and familiarize all members of the family with the steps to take in case of emergency or illness. Being prepared will reduce the trauma brought on by experiencing a health emergency in unfamiliar surroundings.

NEW LIFESTYLES

Household Help

If you are moving to Southeast Asia, the Indian subcontinent, Africa, or Latin America, household help will very likely be available and relatively inexpensive. If you expect to hire household help, this section is for you. Even if you do not, we suggest reading it anyway since it reveals much about cross-cultural relations—and you may change your mind!

Westerners have had little experience in managing and living with servants. Having a cleaning lady once a week in New York, London, or Stockholm does not prepare you for a retinue in Sri Lanka. Household help are an integral part of the social structure in many countries and viewed as essential. Foreigners are expected to have them. You may feel that it is demeaning for people to be classed as servants, and you may not want to enter into a servant-mistress relationship. Nevertheless, there will be pressures to hire help, and life will be easier if you do. You may, in fact, with complete justification, feel you need servants. How can you make the right decisions on this crucial matter?

Try to rid yourself of any feeling that it is demeaning to be a servant. Servants play an important role in the social and economic life of many, many countries. Their occupations are respected and provide employment and status to large numbers of people.

Be wary of household help who appear at the door unsolicited. Word travels quickly that new foreigners are in town. You can be inundated with prospective staff armed with reams of references which are sometimes genuine, but sometimes have been manufactured by the scribe in the bazaar. After deciding on the number and types of servants you need, you face the challenge of living with them. How do you develop amicable relationships?

Communication. Communicating with household staff can be a problem. They want to please you and are likely to nod yes no matter what you ask. You may find, however, that they did not understand at all—with amazing results! Classic examples of misunderstanding abound. You say, "We would like coffee and cakes after dinner," and that is what appears as the guests arrive. Or you say, "We are having special guests tonight. Please make that dish with chicken and biscuits on top." What appears at the dinner table is a chicken casserole with sweet cookies on top (the cook has worked previously for British employers to whom biscuits are sweet). Be gentle but persistent with your instructions. If mistakes are made (and they will be), keep an even temper and a sense of humor. An experienced cook should be given the chance to show what he or she can do before you offer confusing advice. You will probably be amply rewarded by the results.

Theft. You will hear stories of dishonest household help who have "taken" their employers. You will be appalled and tempted to believe the worst. Some of the tales are true, but many are simply rumors or result from the expatriates' ignorance of local customs and of how relationships between employer and employee are managed. Remember that no matter how humbly you live in developing countries, you will always have more or at least be perceived to have more than most of the people around you. Servants are tempted, therefore, to fiddle with the shopping money or cause supplies to "disappear" from the larder, one piece for the pot, one for the pocket. This is known as the "cook's perks." Although this is a well-established method of working in the great kitchens of the world, at least so we are told, when it happens in our homes we get upset and tend to overreact.

There are ways to avoid excessive losses. Keep an account book, entering money given to the cook for shopping. Require receipts for goods purchased and check the change to be certain it adds up. If the staff know that you are keeping an eye on things, they will probably take more care in following the rules. If you are running out of supplies, ask them to tell you before they buy more. If you have access to a commissary or duty-free shop, keep an inventory of the goods purchased there and make this known to your staff. If you have large stocks of foreign goods such as tinned foods, you may want to keep them in a locked cupboard. This is as much for the staff's protection as yours. Be businesslike and the staff will respond. If they do not, there is cause for dismissal.

Keep valuables locked up. This applies particularly to jewelry, money, and important documents. If something valuable is lost, ask your staff to help look for it. Do not assume they are to blame. If it is found, joy will reign. If it is not found, be prepared to believe that it is genuinely lost. If theft can be proved, however, and the culprit identified, dismiss the person on the spot. No arguments.

Salary Advances. One of the thorny issues in relationships with staff is that of salary advances, which can be requested for many reasons. Some have clear justifications, such as the need for extra money for school fees, weddings, funerals, or important festivals. Others do not. A constructive approach lies somewhere between refusing any advance and giving one whenever it is requested. The no-advance approach is fair only if you try to anticipate when needs will arise and give timely gifts. Giving advances whenever requested can only lead to disaster.

Barbara adopted the policy of giving advances within reason but not giving a second until the first was paid off. The advance was deducted from the wages in amounts that would not cause hardship. Nancy has never given advances but pays school fees and helps with house rental costs.

If advances are given, careful records should be kept of how much is paid back each month. Staff members should participate in the record keeping so they understand and do not get confused. Sometimes the paying-back period extends for months, so it is only fair proper accounts are kept.

Be aware of those times when your servants are likely to need extra money—frequently around holiday periods—and provide a bonus. In Moslem countries, for example, people fast from sunrise to sunset during the month of Ramadan, after which there is great feasting—and food prices skyrocket. Staff members do depend on us for financial security just as we depend on our employers.

Time Off. We all have times when we wish the house were empty. We do not want to hear voices coming from the kitchen or the living quarters. We do not want to be followed around the house by the maid carrying out her routine chores. Many people send their entire staff on holiday the same day each week, often Sunday. We have found that we look forward to that day when the house will be "ours," though we have also discovered that we welcome the staff returning on Monday morning.

Family Benefits. When you hire staff, their families may become your dependents. They may look to you for help in times of crisis and hope you will participate in their times of joy, their weddings, births, and festivals. On the other hand, in some countries employers are legally responsible for offering certain benefits to their household help. Check carefully. But even where not required, you cannot avoid your responsibilities in this respect, but you should try to encourage as much self-reliance as possible. After all, when you are gone they may be out of work and have to fend for themselves.

You may be called on to help with medical bills. We feel that if the staff member himself is ill, it is wise to do so if only as a safeguard to your family. When you hire staff, insist on their having, and be prepared to pay for, urine and TB tests and perhaps others as well. Check with expatriate acquaintances. If staff members become ill while in your employ, assist in finding medical care at the sort of place they would go if you were not there. There is usually a local clinic or surgery providing adequate care to which they are accustomed. The treatment should be monitored to make sure they understand it and are following directions faithfully. We have both adopted the policy of helping with expenses for staff members but not for their families unless the staff member is affected as well.

Letters of Reference. When you leave or amicably discharge staff, give them letters of reference. These letters pave their way to obtaining another job and should be written with care. Be specific about the servant's abilities so a prospective employer can read between the lines and determine what the person does not do well. You will learn from your own hiring experience how useful a good letter can be.

Remember to be alert to how your culturally determined attitudes toward "servants" and "service" may differ from those of your household help. These differences can help explain many of the breakdowns that occur.

All of these admonitions and bits of advice are common-sense ways of living with complex human relations; and make no mistake, the employer/employee relationship is a complex one. It can be very rewarding and great fun when you keep your perspective and sense of humor. Use your own best judgment and rely on long-term residents for advice when your own experience does not offer precedents. Household help can add a special dimension to life. We are richer for having known them.

Role Expectations

A move overseas can mean the assumption of new roles. You become the wife of someone who holds a particular position in the organizational hierarchy and are expected to entertain or "appear" or play a ceremonial role at national day celebrations. You cannot forget that you represent your country or company and are no longer just an individual.

Today, the roles we are expected to assume are not so demanding as they once were. Gone are the days when the younger women in organizations were at the beck and call of the boss's wife to serve at tea parties. There is a recognition in all but the most rigid organizations that women are no longer willing to be forced into stereotyped roles.

There will be times, however, when you have to perform certain functions. If your husband is the head of a company, for example, there will be representational entertaining to do. "Have to" entertaining can be a unique opportunity to meet and socialize with friends from the host country. It can be seen as a chore, but, in fact, entertaining overseas is a special experience through which you can express your personality.

Children may feel pressure if they are reminded constantly that their father is important and their behavior will reflect on him. Do not lay a heavy burden on your kids—or yourself—in this respect. Families need to maintain their individuality and live out their new roles in a way that's comfortable rather than burdensome to them. It is, however, necessary to realize that, as a foreigner, you are more visible than at home, and local residents may see you as the typical American, Swede or Australian.

FINAL THOUGHTS ON SETTLING IN

When you first arrive, you need to set priorities: what needs to be done first, second, and so on. Many families get caught up in the whirl of social events too soon after arrival, when full attention needs to be given to getting the family settled and the house in running order. Focus on the practical matters that will make the situation comfortable for all the family members. It is tempting to go off and leave the children while you shop or attend parties, but remember that your children need you and need to have a settled environment in order to make their own adjustments. As a rule, Nancy tries not to leave her child during the first few weeks in a new place and engages only in social activities which include the whole family. There is nothing more disconcerting than leaving a screaming child in the arms of a childminder as you go off to a social event.

Most of all, try to relax during the busy days of settling in. Though the house needs to be organized, it does not have to consume every moment. Take the time to explore and enjoy your new setting with the family. Bare windows can remain so for another day or another week while you explore the zoo or the park with the children. Settling in is an emotional process as well as physical one. Remember that the first days in a new country are the *honeymoon* stage in terms of cultural adjustment and you need to use that time to get out. When you have had a bad day and think you will never get organized, remind yourself of the three- to six-month rule. Don't make unreasonable demands on yourself or others by setting unrealistic goals.

five

Culture Shock

The concept of "culture shock" is not an esoteric one. The phrase, in fact, is simply a colorful synonym for "cultural disorientation" and refers to the reaction we have to being suddenly immersed in an environment which is radically different or new. (It is also sometimes called "change shock" which is akin to the term Alvin Toffler popularized, "future shock.")

The "shock" comes from the fact that the vast range of values, attitudes, and habitual behaviors which guide us and provide us security and certainty in our own social and cultural milieu—and which for the most part we hold or follow unconsciously—are not transferable to the new environment. Different sets of attitudes, values, and behaviors govern life there. The differences are sometimes quite obvious, at other times very subtle. In either case they can cause strong emotional responses—anger, frustration, irritability, resentment, disdain, anxiety, insecurity, and even depression—if something is not done to counteract the disorientation.

When these differences are encountered, two critical questions will arise: (1) How do you react? and (2) What do you do about the disorientation?

Understanding your reaction is important. Half the battle in dealing with culture shock is won if you know what is happening to you. There are some people who seem never to experience culture shock or experience it only in an abbreviated, compressed form, but they are the exception. It is best for most of us to assume that when we go abroad we will experience culture shock in some significant degree.

The culture shock process is often upbeat at first, beginning with the *honeymoon* stage, when everything seems exciting and exotic, seen through rose-colored glasses. It is exhilarating just to arrive, a relief to have that planning, packing, and saying good-bye behind you. You may feel somewhat like a tourist during those first days or weeks, seeing new and interesting sights, being entertained, anticipating the next interesting event—and ignoring the realities of becoming established in your new life.

Would that it could stay that way. But it does not. The honeymoon stage can last anywhere from a few hours to a few months. Most of us are lucky if it lasts a few weeks. In any event, one unpredictable day the rose-colored glasses shatter and reality confronts us and introduces us to the second stage of culture shock, the *anxiety* stage. The newcomer begins to feel bewildered and irritable. Things once described as "quaint" now look "dirty." The market which seemed colorful is now "crowded," "smelly," or "inconvenient." Typical symptoms are insecurity, frustration, and impatience.

Anxiety generally comes from facing problems you cannot define and therefore cannot do anything about. Since the disorientation you are experiencing is over matters which are largely unconscious, it is not surprising that anxiety results.

Simply stated, things don't work. The furniture does not arrive on time, the servants do not understand you, the repairs are done incorrectly, you feel cheated at the market, the directions you give are misunderstood, the directions you get are incorrect, the children want macaroni and cheese (a manifestation of their own anxiety?) and all you can find at the market is a bag of bug-infested noodles, you phone for some information from a friend and get a stranger who doesn't speak English (or anything remotely resembling the local language either). Tension and anxiety mount. You know the saying "everything is going wrong" does not really explain what is happening, but you cannot put your finger on the real explanation. And where are all those new friends who appeared like bees around a jam pot during the first few weeks? Sad to say, once newcomers are initially greeted, taken shopping, and helped to order a few things, they are often left completely on their own—though not with malicious intent. Like people everywhere, expatriates are busy and have their own lives to lead. To the old-timer, the newcomer seems a part of the community long before she feels that way herself.

There is usually another subtle pressure in operation too. No one wants to be known as the person who complains all the time. There is a fine line between "we're helping her get started" and "she's just not adjusting," and the newcomer does not want to cross it. Many feel isolated at this stage, uncomfortable in the local culture and uncertain of their place and the impressions they are making in the expatriate community.

All of this leads to the next stage, *rejection*. A rebellion occurs. Unable to determine what is actually wrong, the newcomer projects her problems onto the handiest scapegoat—the local culture—and develops what is often an intense dislike and even hostility. Typically, the same person who was happily poking around the market and taking her children to nearby parks during the honeymoon stage now shops only in duty free stores, buys Western-style food in tins and packages, and allows her children to play only in expatriate facilities.

There is a tendency to personalize everything negative that happens. The electrician who arrives late or is unable to repair the air conditioner is perceived as deliberately trying to make your life miserable. A traffic jam on the main street when you are hurrying to a meeting is a diabolical scheme designed especially to infuriate you. Things are judged in "black and white" or "we and they" terms. Everything at home is good, everything about this new country is bad. Further, you may not be able to resist the impulse to act out your resentment in juvenile ways, perhaps because in trying to learn a culture you have, in effect, become a child again.

The fourth stage of culture shock is called *regression* and often occurs more or less concurrently with the rejection phase. It is a time of retreat, in which one does everything possible to avoid contact with the local culture and people. It is not uncommon for the stricken person to spend long hours in a "safe haven" (or a closet! see Chapter 6) such as the American Club or other expatriate facility where only fellow nationals are allowed entrance. Contact with servants is cut back severely; in fact, many people, with a teeth-gritting determination to do things their own way, dismiss their servants at this time. Gone are the days of exploring the charming back streets of the city. Language classes begun with great zeal during the predeparture or honeymoon stage are dropped with such flimsy excuses as: "I'll never use the language anyway," or "I know enough to get by."

What brings on this extreme negativism? It can be precipitated by events which trigger inner fears, such as an unpleasant incident in the street or an attempted break-in at the house. Such things make the newcomer feel vulnerable or unwelcome. More often it is a growing sense of being trapped. It hits you squarely that you are stuck in this new country for some period of time. It is not a vacation or a lark. You cannot pack up and go when things get difficult. Hence the tendency to hole up and hope "real life" will leave you alone, at least for a while.

There are people who never move beyond regression, even though they live abroad for years. Others leave during this stage, giving in to the urgent need to get back to the familiar. For most people, however, leaving is impractical. They have commitments to employers, and leaving before a contract is completed is simply not the way to get ahead. Some also have commitments to themselves not to quit. So, for many, sticking it out becomes the name of the game. For others, the challenge of conquering culture shock is the stimulus that drives them on.

For whatever reason, it is at this point that slowly, often painfully, you enter the final stage of the culture shock process, *adjustment*. Adjustment starts as you begin to feel comfortable in your new surroundings. How does it happen? For some people it seems to be simply getting to know their way around.

It is a good feeling to get into a taxi and know where you want to go, how to get there and what it costs. The old rejection feelings that the taxi driver is cheating you tend to magically disappear when you can direct him to your destination. The taxi driver has not changed, you have. You know where you are, which makes you feel secure and thus able to accept others more easily.

Language learning can be a major factor in successful adjustment. Lessons tend to begin again at this stage. You learn to speak enough to work your way around the market and engage in light-hearted conversations with market vendors which help you learn even more. As you are able to communicate with host nationals at different levels, you begin to feel some degree of acceptance and it becomes easier to learn about the culture, its values and its customs, its economic and political realities.

Ultimately, it is learning the culture that is the major factor in your adjustment. You not only know your way about the town, you are beginning to know your way about the culture. You are beginning to understand why people here think and behave the way they do—and it makes sense. It is different from how you think and act, but within itself it is logical and as consistent as any culture can be. Most importantly, you can learn to function quite satisfactorily within the culture according to its rules.

In the end, there appear to us to be two critical steps, or imperatives, in dealing with culture shock and adjusting to life overseas. One is a willingness to view the values, attitudes, and behaviors of your host culture as *different* from yours rather than worse or wrong. Remember, from their perspective, there are no doubt things worse or wrong in your culture also. Until you have developed the ability to examine differences simply as differences, there is little likelihood of achieving the objectivity to judge right and wrong.

The second imperative is self-understanding, or, more precisely, cultural self-awareness. We must arm ourselves with a better understanding of the basic assumptions, values, attitudes, and expectations which govern our own behavior. With that as a tool, we are much better equipped to understand and manage our responses to the unending and inescapable clashes of culture which are part of everyday life in a foreign country.

As examples of what this means, we will look at two basic cultural orientations which have a wide impact on cross-cultural interactions. In doing so we will quote extensively from anthropologist Edward T. Hall, whose first book, *The Silent Language,* is a classic in this field and all of whose books we recommend wholeheartedly to the person wishing to explore the subject further. Hall states succinctly what we have emphasized above, "Culture controls behavior in deep and persisting ways, many of which are outside of awareness and therefore beyond conscious control of the individual."[1]

TIME ORIENTATION

One of the examples Hall uses is time. For the American (to whom his book is addressed), but also to most Westerners, "... time is an element fixed in nature, something around us and from which we cannot escape."[2] We segment and schedule time. We look ahead and are strongly oriented toward the future. Time is handled very much like material: we earn it, spend it, save it, waste it. Promptness is highly valued. If people are not prompt, it is taken either as an insult or as an indication that they are not quite responsible.

It is with this cultural value that a well-meaning Westerner moves to Asia, Africa, or Latin America. Up to this point in her life, it is unlikely that she has ever thought about "time" as anything other than the passing of life and events, or of "time orientation" as a set of culturally determined values.

---

[1] Edward T. Hall, *The Silent Language* (New York: Doubleday, 1959).

[2] Ibid.

Certainly she would be hard put to articulate her time orientation—at least until she encounters others. Then she knows something is wrong. The most common confrontation occurs in the anterooms of business executives, government officials, and other professionals with whom Westerners have appointments.

Not long ago Nancy was asked by a friend to visit the friend's doctor in Jakarta in order to obtain some medical records she needed. Nancy arrived at the office promptly at 4:00 P.M. when the doctor's hours started. At 6:00 he had not yet arrived and Nancy was still waiting, along with twenty-five other women, all Indonesians. Even though she had lived in Asia many years, this "waste" of time still bothered her. The other women, however, were not disturbed. They did not expect him to come on time. He was important and educated and they were only "patients." Waiting for him was a worthwhile use of their time. They relaxed and enjoyed each other. They were participating in an event, not wasting time. These seemingly simple differences in attitude toward time between Nancy and the other women were, in fact, profound. They had been deeply implanted by the long process of socialization each had experienced in her own culture. To change and adapt to the ways of the other would call for great effort and persistence.

At 6:30 Nancy finally got in to see the doctor, who offered a friendly greeting and commenced to chat amicably with her. When Nancy tried to hurry the conversation, thinking of the twenty-five other women in the anteroom, he resisted. To him it was necessary to establish a relationship before he could transact business with her and give her the records.

Thus, another difference in attitude toward time was encountered—time is well spent establishing relationships before other matters are broached, even when, by Western standards, you should "hurry."

Waiting in anterooms is one of the most difficult experiences Westerners, especially Americans, have to deal with in many countries because in their own societies it is considered an insult. In business meetings, the seemingly endless socializing their hosts require can tax to the limit the patience of any straightforward, let's-get-down-to-business American.

Our orientation toward the future can also get us into trouble when we enter a culture where the future is believed to be controlled by fate or by God (or the gods). Conflict is particularly apparent in development fields because the rewards of programs such as family planning are in the future. Planning to have only two children and educate them so that they can provide support in the future is nearly incomprehensible to the traditional farmer. He needs farmhands now and sees clearly the economic value of their coming from his own family. Future orientation is very Western and we need to be ready to see things from other perspectives in countries where ours is not shared.

SPACE ORIENTATION

The idea that people's use of space differs from culture to culture may sound absurd. It is true, nevertheless. Almost without exception, people riding in an elevator, waiting in a queue, or carrying on a social conversation while standing maintain a certain distance from each other. This distance (often called "social distance") is culturally determined and varies from culture to culture.

There are also differences between distances maintained in private and in public. In many countries, people crowd together in public with a great jostling of bodies, touching and pushing. Japanese trains are a legendary example. It is common when abroad to feel that our personal space is being violated. When this occurs, we feel threatened at a very primitive level of awareness. In some cultures—Middle Eastern, for example—personal space begins inside the body so that touching is not threatening. In most Western countries, personal space begins some inches away from the body (sometimes called an "envelope" of personal space) so that touching strangers is quite uncomfortable.

One friend and her teenage daughter who had lived for many years in India were crossing a street in a Western country when the daughter inadvertently bumped into another woman who flashed a haughty "daggers" look at the girl. The mother, in an effort to placate her daughter, reminded her that they were back in that part of the world where people like plenty of space around them.

Understanding our own orientation to space is important. We may never grow to enjoy being jostled, but we may come to feel that we are not being threatened. Barbara's experience on arrival in New Delhi is an example. On her first excursion out of the hotel grounds into a main shopping street, she encountered a "riot" which caused such panic in her that she vowed on the spot she would not stay in India! It was in fact a bus queue! Before long she did not notice these things and was amazed when her visitors reacted in the same way she had.

SHOCK ABSORBERS

How do we as foreigners deal with the cultural differences we encounter? Do we have to sublimate all that we are and all that we would become in order to adjust to and be accepted in other countries? Can we never expect to be met half-way? There are practical issues at stake here. How can a production manager whose bosses in the home office are pushing *their* time schedule work with a counterpart in the host country who is expert at saying *mañana* or *besok*?[3] The expatriate is caught in the middle and hard-pressed to find a solution

---

[3] "Tomorrow" in Spanish and Indonesian, respectively.

that will please the home office and maintain good relationships with the counterparts.

Here are some suggestions. To begin with, try talking it out with your counterparts. Explain the pressure that is on you. Pressure is something that most people understand; there seem to be forces at work, either real or imagined, in all cultures that put pressure on a person and cannot be controlled by the individual. Try not to get angry. Such an easy statement to write and so hard to do! Anger is acceptable in most Western cultures. Shouting, in moderation, is forgiven. Standing around glowering with hands on hips is legitimate. Not so in many other countries. So, if you need to express anger, learn how it is done in your host country.

Be sensitive to your own self and why things are bothering you. Try to remember what the implications are of being a guest in another country. As a guest in someone's home, you must be concerned about your host's schedule, arrive on time for meals, clean up after yourself, contribute what you can to the smooth operation of the household, disappear when there is a personal or internal conflict within the family, and leave if you are no longer welcome or needed. If you apply these rules of being a guest in your host country, you will find that your adjustment and acceptance will be smoother and produce less tension.

The authors of the *Trans-Cultural Study Guide* put the problem of cultural adjustment squarely on the individual when they wrote:

> You obviously can't continue to live as you did in your own culture. On the other hand, it is quite probably not acceptable for you to live exactly as the local people do. You will have to discover your own middle ground. Most likely there will be rules or expectations that will be difficult to follow or fulfill. At times you may choose not to ... A balance needs to be found between maintaining your sense of self and avoiding *cultural imperialism*. Many aspects of yourself that at first seem

essential, may in time seem unnecessary or disadvantageous *cultural baggage*.[4]

You sacrifice some part of yourself to cultural adjustment when you go overseas, whether to teach or to learn. You cannot teach when the learner is angry, tense, or afraid. Nor can you learn when you are unreceptive and trapped in your own cultural bubble. If you are sensitive to what makes your culture special and what is special about the new culture, you can adjust.

Are the sublimation, sacrifice, and learning worth it? Our answer is yes. Edward Hall notes, "The best reason for exposing oneself to foreign ways is to generate a sense of vitality and awareness—an interest in life which can come only when one lives through the shock of contrast and difference."[5]

---

[4] Ken Darrow and Brad Palmquist, eds., *Trans-Cultural Study Guide,* 2d ed. (Palo Alto, CA: Volunteers in Asia, 1975).

[5] Hall, *The Silent Language.*

six

Beyond Culture Shock: The Other Adjustments

Culture shock is a major hurdle to overcome while settling in, but it is not the only one. There are other adjustments to make when you move abroad.

EVERYTHING IS NEW, LIKE IT OR NOT

There is nothing more exhilarating than something new. We enjoy a new house, a new location, even something as simple as a new dress on the right day. On the other hand, everything new at once can be overwhelming. Picture what the first few weeks abroad represent in terms of the "new." In as short a time as twenty-four hours, you are thrust into a new job, a new house, and encounters with all kinds of "foreign" people (actually it is you who is the foreigner). You may have servants for the first time and be expected to speak a language you know only in theory, if at all. There will be strange food, unfamiliar smells, unexplored streets, foreign schools.

The new is often sought after and hard won, but to really appreciate it, it must be made a part of you, integrated into your life. But that takes time. Small wonder that faced with the unfamiliar, children cling to the old raggedy toy or blanket. Children are luckier than adults in this respect, since everyone accepts their need for that kind of comfort, and mothers plan carefully to ensure it. But what about the mothers? In the midst of all this newness, how does she find the comfort and security that children gain from a stuffed animal?

We have a friend who takes some of her "security" with her in her suitcase. To her it is well worth the extra weight to have her favorite pictures and bric-a-brac, whether she is residing in a hotel in Seoul for three weeks or settling into a home in Buenos Aires for three years. She never ships her favorite things, but takes them with her on the plane and arranges them around her even in the most barren of settings immediately upon arrival. Her husband says she has the knack of making a place look like home in five minutes.

We need not copy this friend and carry our mementoes on our backs, but we do need to plan how to make ourselves and our families feel as secure as possible from the first day. The "new" can be wonderful so long as we do not feel we have been cast adrift without anchor.

CRITICAL LIFE PASSAGES

Going through major transitions in life can be difficult enough at home; going through them while adapting to life overseas can be shattering. Some time back, the U.S. Department of State produced a videotape on adjusting to life overseas. In it a psychiatrist pointed out that of the many stresses in our lives abroad, some come from living in a foreign culture and some come from inside ourselves. It is very important, the psychiatrist said, to sort out which is which in order to make adjustments.

We are reminded of a friend who, after years of living in a country where she spoke the language fluently and was professionally employed, moved to a new country. She had a new baby and decided this was the time to stay at home and become a full-time mother. Shortly after arrival, acute depression set in. All at once she had to cope with new surroundings, an unfamiliar language, the loss of professional identity, and a new maternal role. The disorientation, loss of identity, and passage into the critical experience of motherhood were too much. At the time she blamed the new country but five years later readily admitted that her problems came from within herself.

It is essential to our adjustment overseas that we understand and accept where we are in terms of the major transitions or "passages" in our lives and that we have a sense of what we would like to be when we come out of them at the other end.

PERSONAL IDENTITY—WHERE DOES IT GO?

Western women have a strong sense of personal identity. It is manifest in many ways (the use of "Ms." for instance, and the retaining of maiden names after marriage) and was at the heart of the women's liberation movement. This personal identity can be stripped away when a woman moves overseas with her husband, and few women are fully prepared for it. In part, the stripping away is caused by the existence of the old diplomatic/military pecking order—embraced by multinational corporations and other international organizations as well—which prefers that everyone be rank ordered and have clearly assigned roles. A woman goes from being Sally Smith, working woman, community member and organizer, to being Mrs. Robert Smith, wife of Mr. Number Two. What is surprising is not that this shocks us, but that it happens so overtly and we do so little to prepare for it. In the few hours or days it takes to get from hometown to home abroad we are changed from an independent person to a person in a box called "dependent" whose identity, in fact, depends on someone else.

Many organizations like to nurture the "woman in the box" idea. Few of them are helpful to the woman who wants to work or to be something more. They encourage women to be dependent either on them or on the position of their husbands. Organizations may take relatively good care of wives' physical comforts, but do little to reduce the frustration of being dependent, a status clearly indicated by the typical notice in the company newsletter: "Mr. Smith has arrived with his dependents: wife, Sally, and children, Mike and Suzie."

The loss of personal identity comes home to us when new people we meet open conversations with: "What does your husband do?" or, as both of us have been asked, "Are you a wife or a secretary?" People find it astonishing that we have our own reasons for being overseas. We all want to be recognized for our own personal and professional worth, and we have to fight with our compatriots for this recognition, as much or more than we do with the people of the host country.

PRIVACY

Many people experience a significant loss of privacy when living overseas, particularly in Latin and non-Western countries. Westerners tend to need time alone; they carefully cultivate privacy. In many cultures, particularly in Asia, the idea that there is pleasure in being alone is almost incomprehensible. In fact, in many languages there is no translation for the word "private." Joy and contentment are found in the presence of others and in the extended family.

Our sense of privacy may also be violated by household help when we have it. Women who spend their time in the home frequently need to make careful arrangements to insure that some of it is reserved wholly to themselves. Until you become accustomed to having servants around, you may want to stay away from where they are working. You will not bother them, but their presence may constitute an invasion of your privacy, even if you are not conscious of it. Your privacy may also be invaded when you are walking about the market or just down the street. You may be the object of stares, or in some countries, comments and ridicule. There are places where pinching and other offensive gestures are common—

and disturbing to the unprepared. "I can't walk down the street without being bothered," is a common lament from women living overseas.

Our children also experience a loss of privacy. Being touched or pinched by a stranger is as uncomfortable for a child as it is for an adult, even to the point of producing a violent response, such as kicking or hitting. That is sometimes the only way they know how to cope with the situation.

We are advised to stay out of certain areas and to dress appropriately and limit the amount of our bodies we expose. This is advice well taken, but it is also a clear indication of how vulnerable we are to an invasion of privacy if we do not conform. It is frustrating to think that we need to be so conscious of how we appear. After being able to run down the street in jogging shorts without attracting attention, we are thrust into situations where even a sleeveless dress might cause ridicule or harassment.

In general, the simplest way to adjust is to copy what local women wear and watch where they go alone and where they are accompanied. It may be more comfortable to go around with a companion at first. The best advice is to be conservative in the early days until you learn your way around. If you risk too much exposure at the beginning, you may over-react, place too many limits on yourself and develop an intense dislike of your surroundings.

LIVING WITH IMAGES

Wherever you go overseas you have to live with the preestablished images people have of your country and its people. These images, or stereotypes, have been implanted by others who have gone before you and by the products of our cultures which have been sent abroad in large quantities. The images they produce are often less than complimentary and rarely match the way you see yourself. Unfortunately, it is often the worst of our cultures that has been exported: movies filled with sex and violence, lurid stories of entertainment personalities and public figures. It is common all over the world to meet people who are sure that every Westerner is rich, lives in a mansion with a garage stocked with a fleet of expensive automobiles, uses drugs, and believes in "free love."

Women abroad complain particularly of being treated as sex objects. Loungers call out, "Hello, darling, let me kiss you," as you walk by. Women do not invite these comments—or whistles which say the same thing. They come, at least in part, from movies that show Western women as easily available. Nancy had an experience which illustrates this problem. She went to the airport from the office to meet a visitor. She was professionally attired. While waiting she noticed that there was a videotape being shown of a blond performer, clad in a scanty costume, gyrating her way through several sexy musical numbers. The local men were gazing from the video screen to Nancy and back again, obviously associating her with the performer. She felt decidedly uncomfortable.

You are also faced with images of your home country. When something traumatic happens at home like riots, economic depression, or political upheaval, you are expected to know all about it and are held somehow personally accountable for it. Sometimes you will be asked, accusingly, why your country sells arms to your host's enemy. Or in countries where the aged are revered, you are asked why you do not take care of your old people, especially your own parents.

You can overcome these images by understanding the perspectives of your hosts and dealing knowledgeably and sensitively with each issue as it arises, but it takes time and effort. Particularly important is the understanding one must have of one's own culture and society—as discussed in the previous chapter.

DIFFERENCES IN VALUES AND CUSTOMS

In a sense, this subject is what much of our book and certainly most of the chapter on culture shock is all about. We will not belabor the points made elsewhere. There are two customs, however, that Westerners, especially Americans, encounter very frequently and find particularly confusing and/or irritating.

Bargaining. In many countries bargaining, or "haggling," is an essential part of shopping. You are not expected to pay the price asked, which is often twice or even three times the going rate. Many people who go to "haggling cultures" find this one of the most uncomfortable aspects of their new lives. Others take to it easily and carry the habit back home with them—where it often works just as well! The best preparation for bargaining is to have some idea of the going rates. As a rule of thumb: offer half of what is asked and then dicker up from there until you find the "real" price (but beware, this may not work everywhere). In most haggling cultures bargaining is a game or sport; it is considered an enjoyable part of the social process. Play the game; feign disinterest or leave and return with a new offer. If, in the end, you feel you have been "taken," you can probably console yourself with the realization that the amount of money involved was relatively insignificant.

Baksheesh. In many, often poorer, countries, the giving of *baksheesh,* which some call tips and others call bribes, is also a common practice. Here again one needs to ask long-term residents what is acceptable and when. In some countries it will be blatantly asked for, perhaps by the man who comes to repair the plumbing or the boy who delivers the new chair. A small amount will satisfy. In other places, it becomes a more complicated problem—the bit under the table to get a job done on time or secure a seat on the plane—and it will help you to find out early on what the customs are.

LOOKING DIFFERENT

In countries where your physical characteristics (skin color, physique, facial appearance) mark you clearly as different, you may feel a discomfort you have never experienced before. It takes time to get used to being different, to knowing that you will be stared at no matter how conservative your dress or unassuming your manner.

One of our friends told us of a chance visit she and her husband made to a remote village where they stopped to ask directions. The car was immediately surrounded by friendly people. They were delighted to help, but while they gave directions, they grabbed the hair on the man's arm; it was so different from their own hairless arms. The press became alarmingly heavy, but the crowd parted as they revved the engine, and they were followed by friendly shouts and waves as they drove out of the village.

There is little we can do about our physical appearance. Once you understand why people react to you the way they do, you will probably feel more comfortable and perhaps learn something from the experience of being in the minority.

STATUS OF WOMEN IN THE HOST COUNTRY

In one country, the structure of the society was described to us by a national in this way:

> The most respected men are those who are doctors, then come teachers, then other professional men. Farmers are next and finally laborers. People who have the least respect are those who have no employment to occupy them and thus are parasites on the rest of society.

"Where do the women come in?" was our innocent question. Somewhere below the parasites was the answer.

Whether we like it or not, the status of women in the

countries we go to will have an impact on us. If the streets are devoid of women, if women are conspicuously absent from the offices where we work, if we see only shrouded figures hurrying by, it will have an effect on us. What effect depends on what kind of women we are. With our concern for liberation, we may be angered by what appear to be restrictions on women or by the fact that they are highly regarded only when they marry into the right family and have the desired number of sons to carry on the family name.

But we are also affected on a more practical level when our mobility is limited and our acceptance circumscribed by traditional expectations. In some of the Arabian Gulf States, for example, foreign women, like local women, are prohibited from driving cars (even from riding bicycles) and must wear clothes virtually as confining as their Arabian sisters.

Even in less restrictive societies we see women traveling only if accompanied or in modes of transportation designated for them. If foreign women attempt to travel on their own, they may be subject to ridicule. In countries where women gain their status through marriage and childbearing, we find that we do too. "How many sons do you have?" is the inevitable question (daughters often do not count), and it wears on our sense of confidence and well-being.

LONELINESS

"There were thousands of people out there, but I felt alone. There was no one for me to talk to." This is a common lament from people living in big cities everywhere, but the problem is greater when we are abroad. Surrounded, even overwhelmed by people, we are lonely because the old network of people to whom we once turned is not there. We are strangers in a strange land. A secretary with the U.S. Foreign Service expressed it this way: "If I were to give one piece of advice to women, especially single women, it would be, be prepared to be alone and to face yourself."

Loneliness in the early months is almost inevitable. We miss our old friends and have not yet made new ones. Our husbands have their own problems and may not be sympathetic to our needs. But it is also a time for growth as we tap new resources for managing our loneliness and, indeed, "face ourselves."

A first Christmas abroad was a lonely time for Nancy. She and her husband had left the States two months before with high hopes. Several weeks later, her residence just found and still being renovated, her funds depleted because of a bookkeeping snafu in the home office, tropical temperatures sending her constantly to the boiling point, she was not ready for Christmas away from snowy Michigan. Luckily one of the families Nancy met during her first few weeks invited her and her husband for Christmas dinner. Somehow she managed to limp through the holidays and into the New Year. She often looks back on those days and admits that if anyone had given her a ticket, she would have gone home and never looked back. Fortunately, that Christmas dinner revealed the glimmerings of friendship to come.

BAD NEWS FROM HOME

No matter who we are or what our backgrounds, when we go overseas we leave roots deeply planted in our home soil. When we learn that something is wrong at home, the normal stress and anxiety we feel is magnified by distance. We can only rarely fly off and take care of the situation. And even though international communication is improving, it can still be unsatisfactory and frustrating when we are trying to get critical information or comfort a loved one.

As we and our families grow older, the possibility of having to deal with death at long distance increases. In the short course of writing this book, both of us had to cope with the illness and death of a parent or parent-in-law. The decisions that have to be made during such a time are very distressing. Do we go at the first word of severe illness? Do we attend the funeral? Do we go later to help the bereaved? When and how do we grieve when our daily life overseas does not touch the lives of those who died or who are at home?

The best and perhaps only way to deal with bad news from home is to be as fully prepared as possible. Steel yourself to think the unthinkable and decide ahead of time what you will do if it becomes reality.

MEETING THE CULTURE

Husbands and wives—in the traditional pattern in which the husband is the one employed—make contact with the local culture in different ways. The men meet nationals in their offices or other work contexts. Those they meet tend to be experienced with Westerners and able to accept or at least forgive his cultural gaffes because, if nothing else, they value his technical expertise or management skills.

A woman interacts with a different set of people. While her husband is at the office, she is trying to manage the home with her limited language ability, the willing but slow assistance of a new household staff, and her own wits. There is little appreciation and understanding, and no admiration for her managerial skills.

Imagine the potential for frustration in the simple task of planning a dinner. At home, planning would take only a few moments and preparation not much longer. Not so abroad. The smiling cook awaits instruction from "madam" as soon as breakfast is over so he can get the best and freshest buys at the market. Unfortunately, madam is usually not too fresh herself. What follows can either be a protracted conversation covering every aspect of the meal or a hand-waving "Whatever you would like to cook" response. Or take the woman who does her own cooking and shopping. Marketing is not a one-stop supermarket experience in many countries. It is a daily occurrence, and even the simplest meal may require a full morning's excursion. Menus must be planned around available and/or unfamiliar foods; fruits and vegetables may need special treatment. Appliances do not always operate as they should; stoves run out of propane at critical moments. All this takes time and creates frustration. In any case, the results can vary radically from expectations. If the food is inedible, frustration turns to despair.

She thinks the culture is difficult to live in while he thinks she is merely not adjusting well. He is coping, why can't she? It is imperative that they stop and examine their lives from each other's perspective and try to understand how each perceives and interprets the experiences abroad. These differences can be overcome, and you will be able to sit down together at some point later on and laugh at what you have gone through.

LONG WORKING HOURS

Be prepared for a six-day work week, unless you work for an embassy or a development organization. If you work in a host country organization or for a business, you will normally observe local hours and holidays, which in many if not most countries means six days of work.

Sometimes longer working hours are required because the foreign expert does not have trained staff to whom tasks can be delegated, or the number of staff is not sufficient to the task. These situations can result in being married to the job.

Longer working hours can cause stress for the family. The mother and children are left to fend for themselves while the father works twelve-hour days and attends business dinners at night. As one mother said, "There is too much of this country being experienced by only three of us (mother and two children). This isn't what we came here for!" She's right.

A preteen expressed her frustration this way: "My dad is so important here he can't come to my Girl Scout campout. I liked him better in America. He was always home. Now only my mother is."

These longer hours can exact a great toll on the worker as well. A one-day weekend gives little chance to rest. Free time has to be treasured and used selfishly.

FEELING "OUT OF TOUCH" WITH WHAT'S NEW

Hourly news reports, daily papers and weekly periodicals keep you up-to-date at home. No matter how simple or esoteric your interests, sources of new and useful information are at your fingertips.

This is not the case when you live overseas. If you do not have an official or safe mail service, news is old by the time you hear it—if it ever reaches you at all. You begin to feel out of step with your own country and the changes that may be taking place. You are no longer involved in the election process or know much about your favorite ball team. In a tropical country, you can even lose a sense of the seasons and what the weather is like at home. Fads come and go and you have missed them completely.

There are things you can do to remedy the situation. Arrange to receive your local paper, either regularly or in batches. Barbara remembers with great pleasure arriving in California after a long stay overseas to visit friends from her village in England and finding three months' issues of their local newspaper. What fun catching up!

Keep in touch with colleagues or friends who share your interests and ask them to send you articles or books you will enjoy. Subscribe to overseas editions of news magazines. As you think about what you want to keep up to date on, other ideas will occur to you.

TIME—FRIEND OR FOE?

There is a marked increase in free time when you move abroad, especially if you have household help. You can leave the hours of cleaning, washing and cooking in the competent hands of others. This should be welcomed, and usually is, if you have thought through how you intend to spend this extra time. Too many, however, find that they have time on their hands which should be productive, but is not. What do you do with those mornings when your husband is at work, the children are at school, and routine tasks are being done by others? How do you fill the lazy afternoons or the weekends that used to be devoted to shopping, gardening, seeing friends, or organizational activities?

Even if you do not have household help, you find you have more free time because you have left behind old responsibilities and often live in smaller quarters than you had at home.

It is possible to spend whole days, which become months, getting nothing done because you have not yet found what it is that you would like to be doing. It is necessary to manage your time more deliberately than you do at home. A lot of women sit around and mope, thinking about all the things that are wrong with their new home, or spend endless hours in idle pursuits. Others lead very busy, even frenetic, lives but feel empty because the "busyness" does not lead to any goal or give them a sense of accomplishment.

We believe that setting goals is the key to turning time from an enemy into a friend. The goals can be both personal and family oriented. Here are suggestions for goal setting which have been effective for us and for others who have recognized the need to manage their lives better when overseas.

Get the body in shape. Time to work on your flab or your skinny ribs or your heart and muscles is suddenly available. Develop an exercise program, plan a time of day for it, measure your body before you start and work, work, work. The rewards are tangible. You feel better and look terrific.

Stretch the mind. What about taking a college course, either in-country or by correspondence? Or select a subject of interest and pursue it on your own. Find a local tutor or teacher. Ferret out the materials you need in the local libraries, or the two good English-language libraries found in most foreign cities—U.S. Information Service and the British Council. There is no end of opportunity for the motivated person.

Consolidate the family. Living overseas offers more time to be with your children. They will be more dependent on you than at home since many of their normal activities are not available. What is it that you would like to do with them? Become involved in their activities. Do things that bring the family together.

Volunteer. Become involved in helping others (see page 115 for more detail).

Develop a new skill. Many women have become painters, musicians, photographers, or writers while overseas. In Europe, opportunities abound and in non-Western countries new forms of arts and crafts are opened to you. There is nothing to stop you from pursuing hobbies and turning avocations into vocations. It is easy to find teachers and the cost is likely to be less than at home.

Travel and discover the culture. Being able to travel in your host country and to nearby countries is one of the greatest rewards of living overseas. Do it alone if you must, or with a friend or with the family. Plan to spend vacations in a new place each time, learning the history and culture (and even a little of the language) as you go.

We know women who have done all of these things and more. Time became their greatest ally while abroad, and one of the things they missed most when they returned home. Women with goals have a focus to their lives. The time they spend overseas is not time out of their real lives. It is a time for growth.

CRIME AND VIOLENCE

The foreigner is vulnerable to three broad categories of crime: (1) household intruders, (2) street incidents, and (3) political terrorism.

Some organizations offer seminars for outbound employees on coping with crime and violence. Attend if you have the
opportunity. They provide sound advice on how to protect
yourself, though in our experience they are sometimes conducted in a manner that produces much more alarm than is
justified in most overseas situations. If specific information is
not available, the following general guidelines for prevention
and coping may be useful.

Household Intruders. Household intruders can be found
everywhere. You should take the same precautions you would
at home, plus some which are practiced in large cities overseas.
Many homes have metal screens over the outside of the windows on the ground floor. These are often done in pleasing
patterns that allow in light but discourage thieves. High walls
around a compound with barbed wire or broken glass imbed-
ded in the concrete on top are also common. These seemingly
nasty embellishments serve the purpose of discouraging un-
wanted visitors. If other houses in the area have them and
yours does not, you would be well-advised to consider having
them installed. Barbara found her landlord in Kathmandu very
willing to comply. For a while these deterrent features may
be disturbing, but in time you will become accustomed to
them.

Houses should be well lit at night. Lights are one of the
greatest deterrents to would-be intruders. Many expatriates
and host country residents keep noisy dogs. The size of the
dog is immaterial so long as his bark is loud. Firearms are an
unnecessary and dangerous addition to any household. In
most countries they are prohibited by law or require special
licenses to own.

In some countries people hire guards or night watchmen.
Even if the guard sleeps, he is likely to be a member of the
local group of watchmen who watch over the property of all
their employers. If it is common practice where you are living,
hire a guard. In cities where break-ins have been increasing,
some organizations provide homes of employees with burglar
bars, alarms, and other electronic devices. Accept them if of-

fered. Try not to become too preoccupied with worry about break-ins, however. Once you have taken all the precautions you can, worrying will be counterproductive.

Street Incidents. The incidence of street crime is increasing. Where most of the population is poor, it is easy to understand that a large handbag may be too much of a temptation to the desperate urban dweller. An expensive-looking watch or gold chain holds the same allure.

Street incidents can be avoided. All you need are common sense and some knowledge of your new surroundings. In any large city in the world it is not wise to venture alone into areas that are unfamiliar. Do not make yourself a target of street violence by wearing expensive jewelry, carrying inviting handbags, or frequenting alleyways.

Terrorism. In recent years, terrorist activity has increased all over the world. The staff members of embassies and other diplomatic missions, military personnel, as well as businessmen and their families have been targets. Since the taking of hostages has proved to be a productive media event, it is unlikely that their incidence will decrease in the years to come. Urban terrorism is not really new to anyone who has lived in a large city, but it is a frightening phenomenon, especially when you live in an unfamiliar environment. Political terrorism is unlikely to affect you even though it is increasing. Unless you are influential or an important political figure, it is not something to worry over. But there are general precautions which will keep you from being an easy victim:

- Vary your route and schedule going to and from work. This is usually easy and should be a regular practice.
- Travel with car windows closed. Use air conditioning, if necessary.
- Do not look for trouble. If there is local rioting, stay at home. Observe the rules of the country, such as curfews.
- If there is, or has been, street violence, accompany your children to school or keep them at home. Do not allow them in areas where there is trouble.

Terrorism Update

The vulnerability of certain groups of people overseas has increased, particularly the U.S. Foreign Service. There have been several incidents where Americans, specifically, were the targets. But there have also been increased attacks on people from other countries, on business executives, and on general targets (e.g., bombings on aircraft, in airport terminals, or at other public places). These incidents occur most often as acts of revenge by political groups for an injustice which they believe has been perpetrated by a particular country. It seems easier than ever to be caught in the cross fire of political terrorists. Our advice, however, is the same in this edition as it was before. We cannot wall ourselves off or act as if everyone is out to get us. We need to take what precautions we can and then go on living.

Yet we feel it is important to share in these pages what it will be like for those women who are either employees or dependents of the U.S. Foreign Service and its branches. Since the taking of hostages in the embassy in Tehran at the end of the 1970s, the U.S. State Department has made a concerted effort to ensure the safety of its employees and their dependents. While the increased security measures are considered wise by many, there is no doubt that the way "official" Americans live and work has changed.

Guards employed by the embassy security service are now stationed at the homes of American officials and at establishments such as recreational centers and cultural exchange offices. Homes are also equipped with burglar bars and alarms. Many homes have designated "safe havens" in case of attack. In some countries where telephone communication is inefficient, employees and dependents carry two-way radios to keep in touch with each other and with the embassy. Embassy compounds are patrolled by armed guards, swept constantly by closed-circuit cameras, and equipped with gates reinforced with concrete and metal spikes. Embassy visitors are allowed to enter only after their identity is established and they and their bags and briefcases have been searched.

Foreign Service families attend a workshop (now entitled "Security Overseas Seminar" or "SOS") prior to departure and participate in a security briefing as soon as they arrive at post. This is designed to prepare them to deal realistically and comfortably with security issues.

Specific cases of terrorism are responded to with very stringent restrictions. For example, the halls of the international school in Manila are patrolled by armed guards. In Peru, children comment that they cannot even walk a few blocks to another friend's home.

The result of living under these conditions is that the official American community is often set apart, not only from the local community but from other expatriates. Women who are moving overseas for the first time in these days of intensified security as well as women who are accustomed to the easy-going expatriate lifestyle of years past must make a special effort to learn to live with the restrictions and requirements placed on them by their sponsors. It helps to keep in mind that those requirements are designed to save lives.

Our advice to women in difficult security situations—especially if they must remain in them—is that they work as hard as possible at balancing their negative feelings with positive experiences with local people either at work or in social activities. If it is impossible to achieve that balance and if they are in a position to make a change, it is time for reevaluation. After all, women go overseas with certain goals in mind and look for personal growth in the cross-cultural experience. If the situation engenders little but fear, the opportunities to reach these goals are lost.

THE NURTURING ROLE OF WIFE AND MOTHER

Your traditional nurturing role becomes more difficult to carry out when you move abroad. Everyone in the family is working on adjusting in one way or another, yet there is the expectation that the woman of the family will remain a tower of strength, that somehow she'll come through even though she is hurting as much as anyone else. How do you nurture when you need to be nurtured?

Jane and her husband are parents of three teenagers. They moved overseas during the children's preteen years. The move was one that the family had agreed upon and anticipated with joy. They did everything they could think of to get ready, including language study for everyone and trips to the library to gather information about the country they were going to. Despite all this preparation, one child went into a severe depression almost immediately upon arrival. After school each day he would come home and shut himself in the closet. From this safe haven, he would send notes out to his mother telling her how much he disliked living there and how badly he wanted to go home. Jane talks poignantly about those days (they lasted six months) and about the soul-searching she had to do to find the strength to send back into the closet notes that were positive about the experience of living abroad. There were days, she says, when she wanted to crawl into the closet with her son. Yet her husband was so busy at his new job that it fell mainly to her to manage the agonizingly slow process of gaining the boy's confidence and enticing him out of the closet.

Retreat is all too easy in the face of the stress involved. We have known many women who shut themselves into their own versions of Jane's closet—an air-conditioned bedroom or an expatriate club—emerging only to sup with the family at the end of the day. One of the best writers on the subject of East meeting West, Ruth Prawer Jhabvala, has captured the feeling beautifully in *An Experience of India:*

> Of course there are other Europeans more or less in the same situation as myself. But I hesitate to seek them out. People suffering from the same disease do not usually make good company for one another. Who is to listen to whose complaints?

. . . So I am back again alone in my room with the blinds drawn and the air-conditioner on. Sometimes, when I think of my life, it seems to be contracted in this one room, and it is always a very hot, very long afternoon when the air conditioner has failed.[1]

It is a challenge to nurture your family and keep family traditions alive. Women do it in many different ways. One friend plans family dinners with candlelight and music, no interruptions allowed, for every Friday evening. Other families observe holidays in the same way every year, no matter how hard it is. We remember a Jewish family living in a country where conditions, for them, constituted great physical hardship; yet they managed to prepare their traditional holiday foods. Somehow the lights of the Hanukkah candles burned more brightly and the traditional prayers meant more to them there than in any other place. A Chinese-American friend went to great trouble to maintain family traditions. Since cooking was her specialty, it was not unusual to see a duck drying from the ceiling fan as she prepared it Peking-style for her family and friends.

Women do need the support of others in order to nurture. Early on in your stay, you need to seek out women of like mind, who have children the age of yours, who can help you through the rough days. Help is usually available but it is rarely standing on your doorstep; learn to ask for it.

KEEPING CONFIDENT

There are pressures overseas which can squeeze women into one box or role. You have to be confident enough to say that you will be yourself first. We see women who feel they

---

[1] Ruth Prawer Jhabvala, *An Experience of India* (London: John Murray, 1966).

must please the boss's wife, so they appear at luncheon parties or teas when they would rather be mucking about in the garden or playing with the baby. Still others, following the pattern set by old-timers, end up with a complete household staff they do not want because "that's what everyone does." If it is not what you want, why do it to please others?

Don't lose your confidence in yourself and in what you think is best for you and your family because you move into a new setting. Be proud of your skills, whatever they are, and use them well.

seven

Women Who Work

The number of expatriate women working or looking for work overseas has grown rapidly over the years. We find ever more frustration among those who live in countries where government regulations prevent their working outside the home or whose work opportunities are restricted by frequent moves or who are otherwise prevented from obtaining employment.

There are many factors, excluding gender discrimination, which are beyond our control and which affect the prospects of employment:

- Economy of the host country
- Level of overseas aid from your home country
- Employment rate of the host country
- Attitude toward women working outside of the home
- Agreement between the home country and the host country regarding the employment of more than one family member

Experts in the field of career planning have identified certain kinds of professional or career orientations as most suitable for transfer to another location. Francis Bastress in *The Relocating Spouse's Guide to Employment: Options and Strategies in the U.S. and Abroad*[1] calls them "portable" careers

---

[1] Francis Bastress, *The Relocating Spouse's Guide to Employment: Options and Strategies in the U.S. and Abroad* (Chevy Chase, MD: Woodly Publications, 1986).

with the following as the most viable: counseling, health care, secretarial, social work, teaching/training, and writing/editing.

Even if a woman has been pursuing a portable career, she will not necessarily be able to work at it overseas. The United States has reciprocal work agreements with only twenty-three countries (called "bilateral" agreements) which allow dependents to work. They also have what are called "defacto" arrangements with eighty-eight countries which vaguely authorize dependent employment, but are easily by-passed. (See Appendiix B for more on these agreements.)

There are other reasons: local regulations may prohibit two people from the same family working for gain; the dependent may not be sufficiently fluent in the local language to get the job or do it effectively; tough or tricky examinations may be required; it is forbidden to replace a local (this latter is especially hard on those seeking volunteer work; see Chapter 8).

Case in point: in one small country, the international school, because of the bias of an administrator, does not employ dependents as teachers. There are no other opportunities for women to teach in formal institutions there. Although they can tutor local people in English in both formal and informal settings, this is not satisfying professionally for a woman who is trained to teach in an elementary classroom or to teach biology or geometry in high school. In small countries (or countries with a small expatriate school), there might not be any jobs for incoming spouses who are teachers. Even if local hiring policies are flexible, there simply may not be enough slots for all qualified teachers.

Women trained in highly specialized technical fields such as computer programming often find that there are no opportunities for work in countries where there is a lack of sophisticated technology. Unless they are hired specifically to help upgrade such technology, they will probably find no jobs commensurate with their abilities.

The job market in most developing countries gets more competitive every year. More and more local people are educated or trained to do the jobs which have been done in the past by expatriates. Most countries have become increasingly adamant that no expatriate compete for a position which a local person is trained to do. Although those who work in development are pleased to see this happening, it does mean that there are fewer jobs for dependent spouses, an unexpected result perhaps of technical development.

It is not all doom and gloom, however. More employers are listening to the spouses and asking questions as well. More managers are asking about the spouse's expectations before the wage earner is committed to going overseas. More managers are expecting the spouse to come and speak with them about work opportunities. Although managers who assume a spouse will be content with bridge parties and coffee mornings while abroad still exist, they are becoming a rarity.

Yet many women who have a dependent status are finding professionally rewarding work. There are also an increasing number of working couples (called tandem couples) being hired by organizations like the U.S. Department of State, the United Nations agencies, and private foundations. The number of women going overseas as primary wage earners with dependent husbands and children is also increasing. Single women continue to pursue careers abroad as they have throughout the years and in a much wider range of fields. Thus, despite the restrictions, women continue to find employment and other rewarding work overseas. We will explore in this chapter a number of the central issues involved in that effort.

WORKING WIVES

Starting Over in a New Country

Many women look on the move as an opportunity to change their professions or add new dimensions to them. They start over and learn in the process. One woman who taught art design for many years now lives in a culture where the approach to art and design is radically different. She has once again become a student, using her skills as an instructor of design to analyze the design forms in her host country and create something new. When she returns home, she plans to use this new knowledge and these newly developed skills to give her students a broader perspective on art and design.

There are nurses who became nursing instructors, doctors who set up clinics and even operating rooms abroad, and lawyers who became students of local law and then consulted with expatriate companies seeking contracts in that locale. Women who want to start over find many possibilities to develop a new skill or to cultivate a latent one.

There are also disadvantages to starting over. Job continuity is virtually nonexistent. A man gets a promotion or develops his career each time he moves. His wife does not. If the husband takes a two-year contract, by the time his wife has the household settled (three to six months) and finds a job (usually several months), she is effectively working for only a year before the contract is up.

As working wives, we sometimes envy our husbands' professional opportunities and the ease of their transitions. Just once it would be wonderful if there were a job waiting for us. Just once we would like to be paid a professional salary for the work we do—*while* we are doing it. Deferred rewards are fine ("You can turn your experience overseas into professional promotions and high salary demands when you return home"), but they are not always enough.

We speak from experience. Nancy is now in her fifth country. Her husband gets regular salary increases, better positions, and the other rewards which accompany putting in time and doing well. He can continue in this successful stream until he chooses to change careers, since his organization rewards good work with security. It is not the same for Nancy. Since she works in a development field and lives in developing countries, jobs are available. But there may be a ninety-day consultancy here, pure voluntarism there and nothing in between.

Occasionally there is a position with a development agency which provides a reasonable status and salary. Yet every year at income tax time, the moment of truth arrives. There is no comparison between Nancy's salary and her husband's. As much as she reminds herself that this is not important, that career development is possible through variety and flexibility, she knows it for what it is—a rationalization. In fact, if she ever settles (as opposed to having a tour of duty) in her own country, there will be little chance even to *start* a career which builds on past experience. How many fifty-year-old women with "professional development experience" are employed in home country capitals each year? There are days when a dependent wife is not the best thing to be.

The members of any two-profession family, no matter where they live, must make significant adjustments, even to the point of leading somewhat separate lives. Overseas, the need for adjustments is much greater. At home, couples can be employed in different cities and still maintain some semblance of normal family life. Being employed in different countries is, for most people, extremely impractical if not impossible.

Motivations

The woman for whom the move overseas is a once-in-a-lifetime experience can take a different approach than the person who will be on the road for twenty years following her husband from post to post. For the former, we suggest total immersion in the new culture. She should seek job experience in the local setting that will broaden her marketable skills. If she has been thinking about a career change, she can try it in the new setting and see how it works.

The woman who will be constantly on the move should assess her interests and skills and determine where they can be used in a manner that gives her satisfaction. Working in the local community as she moves from post to post may require more time for language training and cross-cultural adjustment than she has. Offering her professional skills to the expatriate community might be a better alternative. Another would be to develop skills that "travel"—photography, clothes design, writing. A little imagination and creativity are helpful in this pursuit.

Most expatriate communities need services similar to those required in any small Western city. There are opportunities for counsellors, teachers, accountants, nurses, doctors, lawyers, and tutors, and the opportunities are roughly the same in most expatriate communities throughout the world so that a career can be pursued even with frequent moves.

Employment Regulations

Much will depend, however, on local regulations governing foreign workers. In some countries, expatriate dependent women are allowed to work if they have a work permit. In others, including the U.S., it is nearly impossible for a dependent to work for pay. If they can, it has to be with the title of apprentice, volunteer, or consultant. In some cases they can work at local salary scales if they can prove their skills are not available in the local market.

Unfortunately, most organizations, while paying lip service to family well-being, provide little information or assistance in dealing with regulations regarding dependent employment. Some women have been told categorically that dependents cannot work only to find that, in fact, they can, by securing a certain license or permit. Whether you choose to work in the expatriate or host community, making potential employers aware of your skills and availability is not easy. Finding a job in a new country is really no different from finding one in any large city at home. "Pounding the pavement," sending out resumes, and calling for interviews are the sine qua non. Know the value you place on your skills and what you want before you apply.

Hiring Practices

As dependents we are easily victimized by unfair hiring practices. How often we have heard an employer say something like: "Well, you are here anyway and would not be working without this job. So you should be willing to work for less." This nonsense is demeaning and more than one woman has given up in the process, only to discover later that the same organization hired a consultant from the home country to do the job and paid three or four times what she was offered.

Nancy had this experience. She was asked by an organization of the host government to act as a consultant on a binational contract. She had lived and worked in both countries and was considered a "sole source" for this job. The consulting fee was to be paid through the development agency which employed her husband. She provided a resume and salary history and reached the final stages of negotiation. Her consulting fee had been established in an earlier meeting, based on her past earning history. All was set, or so she thought. Then the gossip began and people would say to her such things as: "You really think you're worth a lot, don't you?" Several weeks later Nancy was called back to the contract office and offered a much lower fee than previously agreed upon. "Don't forget," said the contract officer, "you are a wife and should consider yourself lucky to get the job at all."

This sort of thing happens often to women overseas. We sometimes despair of its ever changing. Expatriate nurses, for example, have been offered U.S. Foreign Service medical unit nursing positions in overseas posts with the expectation that they would accept a salary less than what teenagers were being paid to teach English to drivers and clerical staff. This situation may sometimes be due to local hire restrictions but the reason too often given is, "They should be happy to have a clinical nursing position in this country since they cannot get a license to practice locally."

The arrogance of the employer is the hardest part to

accept. Most professional women would rather not sit home idle. But they should not have to put up with being demeaned merely because they are in a situation which limits their professional options.

Corporate and Organizational Attitudes

In most expatriate communities, the prevailing attitude toward women who want to work is negative. Some embassies, in particular those of the U.S., try to fill a variety of administrative/clerical jobs with dependents because of complex regulations and quotas on hiring directly from the States. Teachers are pointed toward the school for expatriate children. If your skills fall outside these areas, however, you're on your own. Some corporations and agencies actively discourage you from seeking or accepting employment. This attitude has spawned so much frustration that, more and more, women choose not to accompany their husbands at all. One woman went home when her husband's company ordered her to quit a job (which it had taken her a year to find) due to "conflict of interest"—the company purchased some supplies from her employer.

A banker at a dinner party mentioned that his bank was short-staffed. He had trouble recruiting men to come over. "Why?" he was asked. "The wives are giving us trouble," was his exasperated reply. "They all want to keep their careers. You know what New York women are like."

It has been suggested frequently that employing organizations should take an active interest in dependent career development. Some people want them to guarantee jobs for spouses. Experience has shown, however, that when organizations assume that much responsibility it usually causes as many problems as it solves. It is especially embarrassing when the dependent, for personal and/or professional reasons, has to turn down the position offered—as sometimes happens.

Though we do not like the idea of organizations actually finding jobs for dependents, we believe they should be ready to help. They should be conversant with local regulations and customs. They should be willing to assist in obtaining work permits. They should advertise any professional positions they have open so that members of the expatriate community will know of their availability. Women abroad find that over and over again they are not even considered for jobs they are qualified to fill. Organizations will go to great trouble and expense to hire a short-term contractor or consultant from the home country and overlook the resident woman (because she is dependent or is right under their nose and therefore not so good as someone who is brought in) who has the professional qualifications, is familiar with the customs and language of the country, does not have to be transported or housed, and can be immediately productive.

Almost equally frustrating is the condescension exhibited by organizations which hire women as a favor or to help them out. Overseas offices of corporations and government agencies tend to be even more conservative and traditional than headquarters when it comes to dealing with women in a fair and straightforward manner.

Women who go overseas today require more career satisfaction than women have in the past. Of the 170 women who responded to a survey conducted by the American Women's Association in Jakarta, all but two had college degrees and many had done graduate work. The president of the Association has a Ph.D. Are these women realizing their potential? Of course not! Would they like to have productive work? Most would.

THE WOMAN AS HALF OF A PROFESSIONAL COUPLE

Joint Assignments

Some organizations are beginning to seek out couples to hire; the United States Information Agency, the U.S. State

Department, the Agency for International Development, and the United Nations agencies are examples. This practice has been increasing and the procedures improving so that assignment to the same country is more readily assured by the hiring agency. But there are still problems which justify the comment of one woman who said flatly, "Joint assignments are horror stories!" Someone must always compromise. The employing agency may want the husband or wife and then have to find a place for the other. Some bizarre assignments result and the same degree of welcome is not necessarily extended to both individuals.

Personal issues also create serious problems for such couples, particularly if both are expected to begin working immediately after arriving at post. When they have children who need to be settled, it is particularly difficult for them to give full attention to the work they are required to do. Sending agencies have still not addressed the settling-in problems of these working couples.

Professional couples can spend an inordinate amount of time figuring out possible assignments. Usually they must confine their choices to large countries where more jobs are available. Sometimes accepting a promotion becomes a very difficult decision since it might leave one partner unemployed.

Problems of Household Management

As a rule, organizations which hire couples expect both to be at work the day after arrival. Settling the house and family becomes a hectic process. There is little time for cross-cultural adjustment, language learning, or simply getting to know the neighbors. When children are involved it can be particularly stressful. Think back over what we have discussed in this book and it should be clear even to those who have never lived abroad that the potential for difficulty is great for a couple or family in which no one has the time or freedom to oversee the settling-in process.

Getting Around in the New Country

Some professional couples find that their social life is very narrow. This is particularly true when they have children. By the time they have put in a full day at work, spent some time with their children, or attended a required social function, they have neither the time nor the energy to explore. They have little contact with the country or its people except for an occasional foray to the market on weekends or a trip to a point of interest on vacation.

If there are no children, life is less hectic. But even then, logistics are a constant source of frustration. The stores are open only during office hours. The registry to find household help is a "mornings only" proposition. Other women who are not working may be happy to show the professional woman around but "mornings are best because the children are in school." "Saturday is out because the kids have soccer." So the professional couple, not wishing to be a nuisance, are usually on their own.

COMMUTER MARRIAGES

In Chapter 2, "Making the Decision," we addressed alternative solutions to moving the whole family. We now have a term, "commuter marriages," for what we identified in that section as "alternative lifestyles." Commuter marriages are becoming more and more common, both domestically and internationally, as couples realize that they cannot both pursue their careers satisfactorily in the same place or that they want the children to be educated in their own system, which requires that one partner stay to see this through. It may also be that the parents of one or both partners need care and attention, and one chooses to stay at home to attend to them. For whatever reason, the number of commuter marriages is increasing, and sending organizations must recognize and deal with them in a sympathetic manner.

The positive changes mentioned above—for spouses, tandem couples, and single women—reassure us that organizations and individuals will continue working toward more professionally rewarding conditions for the people they hire and their dependents. Sending organizations are finally realizing that if they want a productive employee, they must do what they can to pave the way, particularly for women who want to follow their careers.

THE WOMAN AS THE PRIMARY WAGE EARNER

More and more women who have dependents are moving overseas. The house-husband of the Western world has become a part of the expatriate scene as these women accept jobs abroad and bring dependents.

Both the expatriate and local community have difficulty accepting the male dependents. A man who decides to follow his wife wherever her job takes them is still suspect, and there is much concern about his happiness.

A few years ago a woman who was assigned to the country where Nancy was living wrote an early inquiry letter outlining her husband's interests and asking if there would be job possibilities for him. Immediately, the male community moved into action and left no stone unturned in the search for job opportunities. Clearly, "he would not be happy in the house all day!" Finally, at a dinner party, the women (all professionals who were looking for or had found their own jobs) exploded. Why all the concern for keeping a husband happy and employed? What about us? Did anyone do this plotting and planning before we came? There was uneasy laughter but the search continued. When the man arrived, he was provided with all sorts of assistance and was successfully and gainfully employed throughout his stay in the country.

Whether a couple in this situation has a smooth transition or a rocky one depends largely on how they organize their lives. If the woman wage earner is also the primary manager of the home, she will have a problem juggling her time and will face the same difficulties settling the household and the children as women who constitute half of a professional couple. If the husband manages the home and children, she will be able to concentrate on her work. They will then experience the same adjustments as the traditional couple, though the husband may have to be more creative in discovering activities in which to participate. If they have chosen this lifestyle and are comfortable in their roles, they can manage their adjustments as any couple does.

SINGLE WOMEN PROFESSIONALS

The increasing number of single women professionals coming overseas reflects the changes taking place in our own societies. Many more women are professionally mobile and choose to become involved in careers which take them to all points of the globe. Some organizations, in response to the women's liberation movement and to new laws concerning equal opportunity employment, actively seek professional women for work overseas. So there are now scores of such women living in every corner of the world employed as heads of organizations and diplomatic missions and in all ranks of development agencies. The business world is still behind in its placement of women in top jobs, although it is catching up, especially in banking and in tourist industries such as hotel management. What special problems do they face?

Social Life

Developing a satisfying social life presents problems unique to this group. Some of the problems are superficial and relatively easy to overcome; others are profound and difficult, often related to culture-based attitudes toward women. Single women often find themselves left out. They are working during the day, so there is the practical problem of finding ways to meet other women outside the office. Also, their mobility may be limited by practical constraints, such as hesitating to travel alone in areas where they feel unsafe or uncomfortable.

Hostesses often find single women difficult to work into their invitation lists. Single women overcome this problem in a variety of ways. One vivacious friend did it by becoming a renowned hostess. She was an adventurous gourmet cook and invited a variety of singles and couples to her home for dinner parties. People delighted in her invitations, never knowing which country's cuisine they would enjoy. The more she extended herself, the more she was included in other people's social lives.

Single women band together and socialize as a group or become involved in local professional women's organizations. Others join clubs to pursue anything from exercise to computers and organize their social lives around them. A single woman has to work harder at finding friends and seeking a place in both the expatriate and local communities.

Casual dating seems to present a particular problem for both single men and women. Dating host nationals in some traditional societies is nearly impossible unless there is a marriage plan first. Dating expatriates can be just about as difficult unless the community is a very large one. There are no easy ways or special places for singles to meet. We have not seen the equivalent of the singles bar or club in any non-Western country of our experience. Many women wish fervently for a simple, casual dating relationship without strings. It's not easy.

Although the gender discrimination that single women have faced has not disappeared, it is diminishing as local people become more accustomed to their presence. Their freedom of movement is still restricted in many countries, particularly Islamic nations, and the expatriate community still does not do a very good job of including single women in its social activities. One single friend pointed out how this varies from post to post: in South America she was treated like "auntie" to all the children and felt very welcome; in her next post, which was "family oriented," she was odd person out and invitations to dinner at her home were not reciprocated.

For the increasing but still relatively small number of single women with children who work overseas, life can still be difficult. In most posts, there are no special supports to accommodate the needs of single parents. As in the case of the tandem couple, the single woman is expected to begin work immediately and will have problems settling in. Both the employer and the children feel neglected.

Inner Resources

Single women have to rely much more than other expatriates on their inner resources, both during the adjustment period and throughout their stay abroad. When a married person has a bad day at the office, he or she has a supportive spouse waiting at home. The circle of love they share helps alleviate the problems of the day. Single women usually come home to an empty house, as they would anywhere, but in an overseas situation, other outlets for relieving frustration and tension may not be available. At home, a woman might regain her sense of humor by jogging, going shopping, watching television, talking with family or friends, or going out for dinner and a movie. These attractive options are not always available overseas. Until she finds a support group, or the right club to join, a single woman will be solving her problems on her own.

Getting Things Done

Another problem for single women is getting things done outside the office. Our single friends lament the lack of time to care for personal and household matters. They have a hard time getting settled, since their employer is not sympathetic to their taking office time for curtain shopping or unpacking air freight. These practical details have to be taken care of in order to create a home. Unfortunately, little accommodation is offered by their organizations. Single women find that their weekends are filled with mundane shopping and household errands, rather than meeting people or seeing something new.

Status of Single Women in the Country

In the social and professional sphere, the single woman is particularly affected by the status of women in her host country. If women are expected to follow traditional patterns, a single professional immediately stands out and is seen as a curiosity. She may be pitied (because her father did not provide her with a husband) or viewed with suspicion (because she doesn't appear to want to have a family). One woman asked wearily, "When will they [her coworkers] stop asking me when I am going to get married? If I say never, they become upset. Why can't they accept that for right now I am married to my job?" Her coworkers cannot accept this because it goes against everything they were taught by their culture about the role of women in society. It is beyond their powers of imagination to conceive that a woman could be satisfied with a life which does not include a husband and children.

Women who have learned to handle the marriage question well do so with a sense of humor and a flip response, such as, "Oh, yes, my father was very lazy and did not get me married off in time. Now I'm too old for eligible suitors!" Any Asian worth his salt recognizes the problem of a headstrong daughter and, laughing also, will accept the reason. Occasionally someone will press for a more serious explanation. Then patience is needed—and keep your sense of humor dry!

We have met single women who find living in very traditional societies nearly impossible. Life is too restricted; even at work, acceptance and success is determined by their sex. If they are content to socialize only with other expatriates and if they can cope with other personal and professional constraints, they can survive the tour. The single woman who wants to do more than survive, however, will have to call frequently on inner resources not often tapped at home.

PROFESSIONAL ACCEPTANCE

One of the most serious concerns of women who work overseas is professional acceptance. While in most societies women can be found in such areas as teaching, nursing or office work, the expatriate woman working in other fields will find professional women on an equal working level in only a few countries. Very often she will find that she does not work with women at all. In such cases, her presence may so disorient her colleagues that they literally cannot "hear" her when she expresses her ideas, responding only to the strangeness of encountering a woman in a professional or executive role. The professional woman must develop a tough skin, be willing to move slowly and cautiously, and have both great self-control and self-confidence.

In a very traditional Islamic society, Nancy was asked by an expatriate foundation to be a consultant to a local development program. The man in charge of the program had spent many years being educated in the West. He greeted her warmly, ushered her into a chair, and then pushed a bell which summoned his colleagues. When they had all shuffled in, he pointed and said dramatically, "Look what the _____ Foundation has sent us for a change—a beautiful consultant!" They looked for a long time, smiled and left. That took care of the first day of work.

In another year and a different traditional setting where there was a veneer of European urbanity, Nancy and her husband worked as partners with equal status (at least from the perspective of the sending agency) on a government project with a large organization for whom consultants were a new phenomenon. The project director was an older man with impeccable manners. Nancy's chair was always held, the door always opened for her; she never lacked for coffee or concern in his office. But at meetings, when, after observing the proper social amenities, Nancy would launch into a description of some aspect of the project for his consideration, the director would stare blankly and in no way indicate, even with the flicker of an eyelid, that he had heard. Yet when her husband took on the role of spokesman and said exactly the same thing, the director's response was warm and profuse. At first Nancy refused to believe that it was happening. But it was and continued throughout the duration of the project.

CASES IN POINT

Here are some experiences professional women have had, both as singles and spouses, while on overseas assignment.

Patricia

Patricia went overseas eagerly the first time as a single woman to be the only health officer in a U.S. State Department post. When a doctor was assigned to the post, people who had relied on her turned to him. When she married the doctor, she lost even more status by becoming the "doctor's wife." When a change of assignment was due, it was the doctor who was reassigned, and she transferred as "dependent." At the new post she was rehired as a nurse, but then with the arrival of her first child she took a year's leave without pay, after which she decided to retire and return to school. But even if she had gone back to her job, the next move would have forced her to start all over again or risk the two of them being assigned to different countries. Patricia has come to terms with the need to subordinate her career to that of her husband, but she is not sure she can continue to do so as the years roll on.

Rita

Rita came to her first overseas experience as a woman looking for a break. She was an educator who worked full-time while having two babies and trying to finish a degree. Her husband's assignment to a country where household help would be available seemed like a dream come true. For the first year she revelled in learning the language, exploring the culture and playing with the children. She did not write a word on her dissertation, nor did she look for a job. During the second year she began to get bored. She dusted off her dissertation, but could not get down to work on it because it was so remote. She went hunting for a job but was offered only volunteer work. She has now decided that as soon as both children are in school, she will take a paying job wherever it is available. Since she and her husband want to keep the family together, they will repatriate if she cannot find professional work in his overseas post.

Maryanne

Maryanne is a homemaker and a nurse. Her first overseas move was with her husband and child. They were in their thirties and her husband was looking for field experience to enhance his career. They are now retiring, having spent twenty years in six different countries. Maryanne has not been able to work as a nurse anywhere. Yet she has coped well. She has taught nursing, developed orientation programs for newcomers, and developed stress management programs for businesses. In all of the countries, she has managed her home so that guests are welcome and the atmosphere serene. She has been the one who has formed support groups for others. Many rely on her judgement and advice. Her ability to be flexible early in her years overseas and accept the fact that she would not be able to practice her profession on her terms was of paramount importance to her adjustment.

The central character in *Stepping*, a novel by Nancy Thayer, sums up the feelings of frustration that professional and work-oriented women often feel overseas:

> It seems impolite and unsporting to criticize one's host country, but then I must say that I don't feel that Finland is a *host* country. It wants my husband here, but it doesn't want me here. It is doing nothing to make my stay here pleasant . . . . My children and I are valueless . . . and no one will help us . . . . The prejudice here is not against Americans or women as such, but against women with small children. And it is such a subtle prejudice: we are simply ignored. . . . And yet it's more than all that, and different: it's me. If I were not so crazily ambitious, if I did not have this itch to teach, to work with words and people, I could be happy here. . . . It is not simply that I am a spoiled American woman who feels seriously deprived without all my electrical luxuries, although that is part of it; heaven knows how I miss *Sesame Street*. It is that I have managed to become competent in a certain field. It is that I want to work.[2]

And yet, despite the "war stories" that almost any woman who has lived and worked overseas can report, for most it is an experience they would not have missed. The efforts made in finding work or career outlets and the challenges involved in doing the job well and in overcoming the hurdles encountered have produced in them personal growth of a kind they would not have achieved otherwise.

---

[2] Nancy Thayer, *Stepping* (New York: Playboy Paperbacks, 1981).

eight

Women As Homemakers

Many women, by choice or because of local regulations, are full-time homemakers while living overseas. There are many reasons for making this choice. In Western countries the pressures on women to enter the work force are great. Women who have worked in their own countries may be ready to take time off in their new environment, searching for some relief from the frenetic life they led as career women, home managers and "supermoms" all rolled into one. They may welcome a year or two in which they can devote their energies to family and home. For others, the economic necessity which drove them into the work force in their own country is not a concern overseas. Salaries and perks for the husband are normally quite generous. Some do not feel they will be overseas long enough to make the search for a job worth the effort. Many women who have been homemakers simply wish to continue in that role.

How do these women manage overseas? What are their special concerns? How have they made living overseas as homemakers a good experience?

TIME MANAGEMENT

In countries where household help is available, time management takes on a different dimension. No longer does the homemaker spend most of her day on household chores, shop-

ping, and food preparation. Instead she supervises others doing the work. It is important to hire people who will do what
you want them to do and allow you to do what you want. If
you enjoy cooking, do not stop because there is a cook in the
kitchen. If your child enjoys the school lunches *you* pack, keep
packing them.

One of our friends has been very unhappy in her time
overseas. She has three children and is primarily a homemaker.
She lives in a country where ample household help is available.
One day before Christmas she dropped in on Nancy to find
her and several children in the kitchen up to their elbows in
cookie baking for the holidays. Chaos reigned as chubby,
clumsy little hands colored frosting and tried to make lumps
of gingerbread look like Santa Claus or Frosty the Snowman.
Plaintively she asked if her children could join in the fun. "My
cook would never let us in the kitchen to make such a mess!"
she said. She had allowed the staff to dictate how her house
would be run and to take over the things she enjoyed. If a
woman cannot go into her own kitchen for fear of offending
the cook, she has the wrong cook—or she has established the
wrong kind of relationships with her help.

Even when you do the things you enjoy in the home, you
will still find that there is a lot of time left in the day. Chances
are the children are being driven to school and are involved
in various lessons and activities. The cleaning, laundry, and
ironing are being done by someone else (unless you really
want to do them). If there are small children in the family,
time must be devoted to them. But if the children are in
school, there is time to spare.

How can you use this time fruitfully? In a large overseas
post, the number of activities going on in any given day or
week is almost mind-boggling. The following is a sample list
from an American Women's Association newsletter in a large
Asian city: "astrology course, book club, choral singing,
bridge, brush painting, cake decorating, Chinese and Indian
cooking, creative writing, bowling, mah-jongg, Raja or
Siddha yoga, smocking, square dancing, stained glass mak-

ing." These classes are being offered by only one of several groups in the city who have similar lists for their members. Here are some examples.

School-Related Activities

There are always programs at the school which need volunteers. There are teams to coach or cheer on, Scout troops which need den mothers and leaders, and teachers who need assistance in the classroom. The library needs volunteers who are willing to read stories to the young children and reshelve books. Possibly the school office needs women who can type to help with classroom material or newsletters. School fairs or bazaars can always use a helping hand. There is no shortage of work in the school setting for the willing volunteer.

Recreational Clubs

Expatriate recreational clubs constantly search for volunteers to plan special events such as Christmas and Easter parties for the children, to work on newsletters, to serve on a board of directors, or to organize tournaments. In many communities, these clubs are the focal point of social life for expatriates. Interaction between clubs in the form of tournaments and special events are often planned by women who have the time—and they develop useful management skills and meet interesting people in the process.

Learning New Skills

Remember the section in Chapter 6 on goal setting? One goal was to learn new skills. The opportunities are endless. You can learn anything from Indian dancing to batik making. Becoming knowledgeable about a particular aspect of your host country can be extremely satisfying. This may mean tracking down information on certain kinds of fabrics, baskets, or pottery and becoming an authority on them. Combining this knowledge with an interest in interior design could lead to your becoming a consultant to newcomers on decorating their homes or even a local agent for exporting the products back home. One expatriate became an authority on Tibetan rugs in Nepal and now runs a business, commissioning the making of rugs and shipping them back to America. Another used her interest in traditional weaving to produce a book on the palace cloth collection of the local royal family.

Even if you do not end up running a business or writing a book, the satisfaction from learning all you can about a particular aspect of your host country can be enormous.

The Performing Arts

Many overseas communities have amateur theatrical groups, choirs, and orchestras. The talents displayed by these groups and the entertainment they provide for the community are well worth the time and effort invested by performers and support crews. Women are often the backbone of these groups, offering both their time and talent. You may have felt diffident about performing at home where there were so many skilled people, but overseas you may be the only person in the area who can play the oboe or violin. Perhaps you enjoy amateur dramatics but never had the time at home to indulge yourself. Overseas you will have the time, and you may, in addition, be very much in demand.

One woman, who had been a professional actress before she married, was carried off by her husband to travel the world. Searching for a way to continue her professional activities, she found satisfaction in giving poetry and play readings. Soon she was in great demand, so much so that she stimulated among expatriates an interest in developing other, similar kinds of performances. One of them consisted of poetry readings with musical accompaniment, which had the added advantage of providing musicians in the community with an outlet for their talents.

There are often choirs which welcome new voices, trained or untrained. Enthusiasm is often the major criterion for joining, so do not hesitate. And remember, your staff will be there to cook dinner and care for the children on rehearsal nights.

Volunteer Work

In many places there are active volunteer organizations, some of which are concerned with the culture of the host country. One of the most sophisticated groups we know is in Indonesia where women, expatriate and Indonesian, began by volunteering at the National Museum and now have a large membership devoted to the study of Indonesian art and culture. Many members who have left Indonesia have started similar groups in their new posts.

There is also the opportunity to do volunteer work in the host community. Many women have worked in orphanages, hospitals, international schools, or schools for the learning disabled. You may have to know the local language, but not necessarily.

There is a need for women to organize volunteer activities for expatriate teenagers in overseas communities. Teenagers overseas have more time on their hands than they do at home and many of them welcome having something useful to do. One ambitious scheme was developed by the mothers of international school students. Their daughters wanted to do something similar to the volunteer work done by hospitals in the States. The program developed into one for both boys and girls who worked in local hospitals and orphanages and helped deliver powdered milk provided by the United Nations.

Doing Your Own Thing

What better place to develop your special interests than overseas. You have the time to perfect that hobby, take those singing lessons, discover the talent that has been lying dormant, waiting to be discovered. Several friends started painting seriously when they moved overseas. Some of them are so good they mount exhibitions and put their work up for sale. Many of them complain when they get back home that they lack the time and space to pursue their painting, and look back on their overseas years with longing.

One young friend had a pretty but untrained singing voice. Overseas she took lessons and has developed into a very fine singer. Another friend decorates cakes in the traditional Western style for special occasions. With six children at home, she had plenty of opportunity to make cakes but not much to make contacts in the local community. She decided, therefore, to offer to teach cake decorating to her neighbors if they would come to her house and speak to her only in their language. They had lots of laughs and some good cakes, and sold the cakes to the expatriate community. But the real benefit was in getting to know her neighbors, learning a little more of the language, and having fun in the process.

Being a Hostess

A person who really enjoys entertaining, from menu planning to table decorating, can expand her skills while living overseas. Many corporate wives and others with entertainment responsibilities spend hours experimenting with new recipes or new ways to handle social occasions.

Polly, for instance, is skilled in using local food to create gourmet dishes. Her dinner parties are anticipated weeks in advance by the lucky guests.

Martha is trained in flower arrangement, which she uses to the great benefit of both herself and her friends. In countries where flowers are abundant and cheap, there are ample outlets for this skill. Think of having someone arrive at your home early on the day of a party laden with buckets of flowers to be placed about your home in beautiful arrangements.

Other women are "born hostesses" and have the ability to create "havens" for others. They take in the "strays" who seem to abound overseas, the short-term consultants, the singles, the men left behind while the wife and children are on leave.

Havens are also created by women who take pride in preserving the way of life they led back home. Imagine the fun we had while living in a large foreign city when we were invited to the home of a friend who maintained all the traditions of an English country home in her small flat. We were formally greeted at the door by the "butler" (small matter that he was clad in local dress) and shown into the living room which was perfectly furnished and full of flowers. The evening progressed in the comfortable surroundings of English tradition as we were cosseted through drinks, dinner, and coffee and brandy. The fact that she could pull it off in an alien country was the best part of it. We could forget for a while that we were foreigners.

Helping Others Do Their Thing

We have been fortunate to know women in all of our overseas posts who have taken the needs of the expatriate community quite seriously. They have eased our lives and those of others simply by caring. These are the women who welcome the newcomer with a cheery smile and a helping hand and follow up with a call after a few weeks "just to see how you're getting on."

There are women who entertain other people's children along with their own. We have benefited greatly from those who have started preschool playgroups in their homes. They were not necessarily trained teachers but rather women with young children who had time and who opened their doors to other children and mothers.

One of our most interesting friends works with host country women developing handicraft skills. She began with friends of her household staff, teaching them to make dolls and other handicrafts to be sold in shops for the tourist trade. When she left the country, she also left behind a flourishing little cottage industry which employed twenty women who were on their way to becoming financially independent. This story is repeated often. Women start a small project from their back door, find that it mushrooms, and have a small-scale business on their hands.

One businessman's wife taught local women to copy designer sport clothes. She assisted them with fabric choice and finishing. There was a ready market among Western women and a full-scale business developed.

The women who teach these skills are to be much admired. These small development projects often show more immediate and tangible results than the large development programs sponsored by governments. The results may not be reflected in the growth of the GNP but are visible to the local people. The rewards for a woman who sees economic growth and development in her own backyard can be deeply satisfying.

Working on Personal Goals

The time spent in an overseas assignment can pass rapidly. You may feel like you have barely got the family settled when it is time to be off again. But these are important years in your life and they should not be wasted. You have to set your goals and work toward achieving them; otherwise you can wake up at the end of your stay feeling you have done little and regretting that you have not changed or grown in some significant way. One friend came to Nancy a few days before her departure. She had heard Nancy speak earlier in the day about overcoming culture shock by setting goals for your time abroad. "Your talk depressed me so," she said. "I have been here for several years and never set a personal goal for myself. Now, I'm leaving and it is too late!"

It is easy to reach that time of regret, but it is not necessary. There are things to do, there are women who have done them before, and there is plenty of opportunity for those who come after.

nine

Special Concerns

Every woman who goes overseas carries her cultural, ethnic, and national identity with her. In some cases this is immediately apparent; in others the differences are not easy to identify. Appearance, individual cultural heritage, country of origin, cross-cultural marriage, and anticipated similarities with host nationals all present challenges that will be explored in this chapter.

COLOR AS AN ISSUE

One of the most obvious differences is color, which can elicit distaste or fear as well as delighted recognition.

More African-American men are moving overseas to work accompanied by their families. More African-American women, both single and married with dependents, are pursuing their careers in foreign lands. People of Asian descent from North America and Britain are relocating overseas in greater numbers than ever before, a trend which is expected to continue as they play an increasing role in professional and technical fields and in military services. The Japanese run multinational development and business projects of all types, and the Koreans are only a few steps behind. The fastest growing group of expatriates in Nepal, for example, are the Japanese, which is reflected in the increasing numbers of Japanese children enrolled in the international school. More sub-Saharan

Africans are joining development organizations, the UN in particular, and contributing to the changing face of expatriate communities around the world.

Do these women face special problems? Often they do. Discrimination does occur in some countries, and it can be painful, particularly for the unprepared. In many Asian countries, dark skin on a native-born baby is considered a disgrace. It is not unusual for native mothers to be ashamed of babies with dark skin and to make disparaging remarks, even of their own children, if they are "too black." Anyone who has ever read the advertisements for brides in Indian newspapers will know the importance of a "wheaten" complexion. Women go to great lengths to keep their skin fair. An Indonesian friend responded to our comment about her seventy-year-old mother's practically flawless skin with a laugh: "What do you expect? She's been in the sun five minutes of her whole life!"

A sub-Saharan African friend had a difficult experience in an Asian country where there was a strong prejudice against dark skin. The ghosts in the children's fables are all depicted as black-faced wraiths with gleaming white teeth. Their most well-known goddess, in her violent form, is always shown with a black face. Hence, as our friend walked the streets of the city, she had to endure screams of fear from children. The adults also kept their distance. She was angry. Fortunately, however, she was able to talk about her situation with a group of women, some of whom were expatriates and others who were natives of the country. The native women were able to explain their religion and fables and talk about prejudices in their society. One woman told of the discrimination she had faced as a dark-skinned child in a conservative and color-conscious family. Our friend was still the victim of fear, but understanding the reasons behind it helped her to be more forgiving. Her life was really changed by the local women who became very supportive, spent time with her, and were, in the best sense, friends. As a result, she was able to balance her negative experiences with the very positive and special experiences she had with the local women.

African-Americans can be discriminated against, or at least held at arm's length, in sub-Saharan Africa. Many organizations, particularly development organizations, began sending black employees to projects in Africa as they rose in the ranks of those organizations. They did this with the best of intentions, thinking that African-Americans would be accepted more readily than white Americans. In many cases, however, there were no open arms to American "brothers" and "sisters." As David Lamb says in his book, *The Africans:*

> The return to Africa brings joy to some Americans, disillusionment for others. But for almost all, whether expatriates or tourists, there are two over-riding impressions: first, the blackness of one's skin does not guarantee immediate acceptance; second, Africa may be the homeland, but the United States is home.[1]

Actually, some Africans have been quick to criticize the United States when it sends blacks, saying that it shows how little Americans think of Africa when they send their own "second-class" citizens to work there; the changing status of blacks has not been well publicized in Africa. David Lamb also addresses this situation:

> ... in many capitals, African government officials are distinctly displeased when Washington assigns an abundance of black diplomats to its forty-two embassies on the continent. At one point in the late 1970s when the ambassador, aide [sic] director, and Peace Corps director at the U.S. embassy in Kenya were all black, a ranking Kenyan official remarked at a cocktail party, "Why doesn't Washington send us its *top* diplomats, instead of sticking us with all its blacks?" ... most Africans are still imprisoned by a colonial mentality, believing that a European—as all whites are called in East Africa—is somehow more capable than a black. This attitude is not surprising when you

---

[1] David Lamb, *The Africans* (New York: Vintage Books Edition. June 1987).

consider that most whites an African encounters are in positions of authority, or at least are involved with missions that
can bring change to Africa: they are doctors, businessmen, diplomats, dispensing justice and money . . . .[2]

Asian-Americans, or Asian citizens of other Western
countries, can also experience discrimination when they go
overseas. This is especially true when they "represent" their
country or are the first to arrive in the host country and do
not fit the stereotype host nationals have of them. It still causes
surprise when Canadian engineers turn out to be of Indian or
Taiwanese origin.

These kinds of occurrences will continue and very likely
increase as minorities go overseas in greater numbers, though
outright discrimination should diminish as familiarity leads to
understanding and acceptance. In the meantime, women from
these groups, both workers and dependents, continue to experience prejudice and discrimination. If, however, they try to
find out the reasons for people's attitudes, they will, like our
friend, be able to balance the negative experiences they may
be having in public places, and possibly in their work setting,
with positive ones involving individuals of the country.

WOMEN FROM SMALL COUNTRIES

"Where are you from?" is the question we are asked
most often. "The United States," "Australia," or "Great Britain" are answers which are greeted with a sagacious nod, a
welcoming smile, or a deep and angry frown. People have
opinions and some knowledge (often faulty but firm) about
these countries. But when expatriates from Honduras or Guatemala, Sweden or Denmark are asked this question, their
answer is often greeted with a puzzled, "Where?" Not only are

---

[2] Ibid.

their countries unknown to many whom they meet, they are often the only representative of that country. Diplomatic missions of small countries may be staffed by only one or two professionals, and this can be a lonely experience.

Because English has become the lingua franca for most of the world, it is a useful language to learn for those who intend to pursue an international career. In some countries, English will suffice for their whole stay; in others, it will allow them to communicate at work and socially until they learn the local language. While those whose "mother tongue" is English can relax at most multinational parties, our friends from small non-English-speaking countries have the wearing, frustrating experience of having to cope with English as well as another culture.

What is even more difficult for many nationalities is that the only suitable school for their children is one where English is the medium, not only in the classroom but also on the playground. Although children usually learn new languages quickly, the intervening weeks or months while they are learning English can be harrowing for both their parents and them. Then when the children do become comfortable with English, they sometimes refuse to speak or study their native language. This is a serious concern for parents who plan to return their children to school in their own country when they reach an appropriate age.

An Israeli friend explained the dilemma. On her family's arrival at their first post, the children, aged eight and ten, spoke no English. For two years they struggled in the international school, taking English as a second language and trying to keep up with their other classwork. Their parents were unhappy that the children were not able to keep up with their Hebrew at the same time. In their second posting they were delighted to find a Hebrew school, but their initial pleasure was soon muted as they realized just how far behind their children were in their own school system and with their own language. The mother lamented, "We have to get them back home soon. Otherwise, they will fail in their own country."

Some families find they must place their children in schools in their home country by the time they are eleven or twelve and certainly for high school or its equivalent. Others choose to keep their children with them at an international school and ultimately apply for university placement in an English-speaking country.

Similarly, while North Americans and Britons will find that their traditions, like their language, are well known in most of the world, this is not true for people from other countries. Santa Claus or Father Christmas in his red suit and snowy beard is an almost universally recognized symbol of the Christmas season; St. Lucia of Scandinavia and Black Piet from the Lowland Countries are virtually unknown.

Many women from small countries seek out others from their country, neighboring countries, or countries with a common language. Some choose to share their culture with others in a positive way. We know a group of Spanish-speaking women from a variety of South and Central American countries including Guatemala, Honduras, Costa Rica and Chile. At first they clung together, meeting often for lunch or tennis. They would be seen clustered together in animated conversation at the international club. Women of other nationalities would stop by and try out the few words in Spanish they had picked up while living in Bolivia or Peru, Columbia or Mexico during their own odyssey. Soon our native Spanish speakers had an idea. They started a Spanish conversation group and invited everyone, including beginners, to join. Now the group converses, socializes, and shares holiday parties complete with piñatas, native dancing, and food.

Obviously, women cannot (and would not want to) change where they are from, nor can they expect local people to know about their small homelands. But women can handle this lack of recognition and attendant loneliness by emulating our Spanish-speaking friends and being prepared to share their cultures and traditions with others. International school programs have been immeasurably enriched by women who are willing to teach the dances or music unique to their countries.

Expatriate communities have shared good times at "national days." Local people are delighted to have the opportunity to share these days and holiday traditions from other countries. Many are curious enough to want to learn the language or study the political system or history. Women open to the possibility of sharing their countries and cultures seem to find creative ways to do so wherever they are.

FOREIGN-BORN SPOUSES

People have been marrying across cultural and national boundaries for many years. Traditionally, there has been a large influx of brides to the United States in the aftermath of wars. Other couples meet at universities around the world, while serving in the Peace Corps or other such agencies, or during a posting overseas.

More and more of these couples are now going overseas to live and work. Informal U.S. State Department sources estimate that about 30 percent of the spouses in the Foreign Service are foreign-born. In recent years, the State Department has developed special programs for this group of spouses, though they concentrate on Washington-based seminars and a support group which assists spouses in their adjustment to American life.[3] At overseas posts these formal supports rarely exist, but when there are enough women from one nationality, they often develop strong but informal support networks.

These women are expected to be just as "American" as their husbands; they are expected to know how to cook a turkey or create a typically American costume for United Nations Day at their child's school. Few understand that the

---

[3] Foreign-born spouses of U.S. Foreign Service employees should contact the Overseas Briefing Center of the State Department when they return to Washington, D.C., for assistance and ask to be put in contact with possible seminars/workshops or support groups.

foreign-born spouse has extra adjustments to make: she has left her own culture, married into a family of another culture, and is now trying to adjust to yet a third one. Most of these women tend to adapt to their husband's culture rather than achieving a balance of both. Unfortunately, this too is difficult. They may receive a cool reception from expatriates from their husband's country, and their less-than-fluent English may further limit interaction. At the same time that they are struggling for acceptance with their husband's people, they are trying to cope with cultural adjustment to the new country. It is not easy.

The women in this group who are the most successful use a combination of strategies to achieve this success. They work hard to accept their spouse's way of life; yet, they try to share their own culture as well. One friend exchanged instruction in preparing an American Thanksgiving dinner for lessons in Vietnamese cooking; another exchanged lessons in her language for lessons in English. Many may be more experienced in shopping in local markets and in effective bargaining techniques. They are often willing to share their expertise and guide others through the marketplace.

As with the others highlighted in this chapter, these women are most successful overseas when they can balance what they have to learn with what they can share. No woman in this situation, however, should force herself to meet unrealistic expectations. Most of our friends in this situation find it is important to concentrate on their families and become comfortable with their husband's language and customs before reaching out and adjusting to the new country.

WOMEN IN EUROPE

Women from countries where the role of women in society is changing rapidly—especially those from Britain and the U.S.—are sometimes surprised and frustrated to find that the people in many Continental European countries are locked into traditional perceptions of male and female roles. Here is a description, from the Geneva Women's Cooperative (GWC) of the situation in Switzerland in 1980:

> Women entering any foreign country are subject to not only the attitudes the host people have towards foreigners but also those they express toward women .... According to a poll taken in December 1980, Swiss men stated that they highly valued Swiss women for their abilities to cook, to keep order, to manage family life and a happy home, and to be enthusiastic, well-groomed, and reliable. . . . Woman is seen as "the cheerful, harmonious other" who exists to serve others.[4]

What is even more surprising to the visitor is that many European women are content in these traditional roles. An American friend who moved to The Netherlands from Southeast Asia was shocked to find far fewer opportunities for work there than in Thailand. She also discovered that the majority of married women in The Netherlands were not even interested in roles outside those of mother, wife, and homemaker. There are other surprises as well, best illustrated by following Sarah's story.

The Case of Sarah

Sarah anticipates a relatively easy transition to Geneva, where her husband is being transferred by a multinational firm. She lives with her husband, their two children, and a cat in an old, rambling house with a large garden ninety miles from London. The distance between their country village and Geneva does not seem very great, physically or culturally.

One of Sarah's most important considerations is whether she will be able to continue her career as a freelance editor.

---

[4] Geneva Women's Cooperative, *With Our Consent?* (Geneva: Geneva Women's Cooperative, 1983).

She starts her enquiries with her husband's employer. Unfortunately, many organizations, even large multinationals, are not prepared to provide this sort of information for spouses. If her husband's is one of them, Sarah will have to contact the Swiss embassy to find out the regulations regarding work permits in Switzerland. As will be seen below, Sarah discovers that the situation in Switzerland is particularly difficult.

Schooling for their children, a boy of seven and a girl of three, is another important consideration, and a letter to the employing organization should elicit information about schools and day care or playgroups. Again, if it doesn't, Sarah will have to find out for herself what is available, or she can pursue one of the alternatives: enrolling her children in a boarding school in England or staying in England with them. As the distance from England to Geneva is not great, it is tempting to think that frequent trips will be possible; however, air fares in Europe are very high, and although deals are available, they usually have a lot of strings attached.

Another potential problem is aging parents, who might need assistance. It is reassuring to know that telephone communication will be relatively easy, but this can also be frustrating, perhaps because they will be so close and yet so far.

Although some familiar stores will be found in Geneva, the prices will be much higher than in England, so purchasing clothes before departure is necessary, especially for the children. Because the cost of medical care in Switzerland is very high, a medical check-up is a good idea, and medical insurance will be essential unless it is provided by the employer. If time permits, a crash course in French will be useful in preparation for coping with emergencies and the process of settling into a new place, especially with small children.

As the time to move approaches, Sarah faces preparations for departure. The move will be considerably easier than a move to Asia would be, but careful plans still need to be made. The family intends to rent their house and store most of the furniture until a place is found in Geneva. A good home must be found for the cat as the Swiss rarely allow pets in apartments, and, in any case, the cat would not tolerate being kept indoors after a life of roaming the fields. They plan to drive one of their two cars to Switzerland, but insurance needs to be altered and spare parts bought if their British car is one that is not commonly driven in Switzerland. The second car must be sold or stored safely.

Finally, the day of departure arrives. As the family drives off the ferry in France, Sarah finds herself in another world, just two hours across the Channel—so close, yet so different. Distance does not govern differences, Sarah discovers.

On arrival in Geneva, Sarah's first order of business is getting settled. The family moves into a residence—a furnished apartment for short-term letting—while they look for an apartment to rent. A house is out of the question—houses are scarce and expensive—so the first adjustment to be faced is that of much less space and no garden.

Sarah wisely seeks advice in finding out about available apartments. Should she go through an agent? If so, do she and her husband pay or does the owner? Is there a deposit/premium, both for the apartment and for utilities? She finds that in Geneva a large deposit is needed for a telephone. How much rent will they have to pay in advance, if any? What is provided in the apartment? Is the kitchen equipped with a fridge and stove? Sarah discovers that apartments in Geneva generally have to be outfitted with such things as light fixtures and suitable flooring before they can move in. Should they expect to sign a lease and, if so, for how long? Where will they keep the car?

Sarah finds that food shopping is also quite different. At the supermarket everything is, of course, written in French—the signs, the packaging, instructions at the check-out counter. Meat is cut differently, the brands are strange, and the weights and measures are metric.

Sarah will most definitely experience culture shock, going through some if not all of the stages we have discussed earlier. This may be exacerbated because she does not expect culture shock to be a problem, or at least not much of one. After all, it's just Europe, not Asia or South America. However, Geneva offers its own particular obstacles to feeling at home. One of the respondents to the GWC study has this to say:

> Because so many of us are international we float here. This city [Geneva] is unlike Buenos Aires or New York. There the foreigner is still a small minority. Those cities surround you. Whether you like them or not, they are something you must adapt to. Here there is nothing really to adapt to. . . . Here one just floats.[5]

Another respondent said in a joking voice,

> "In the village [in Geneva] where we now live they say you are not "one of them" until someone from your family is buried in the local cemetery. I'm not sure that we're that anxious to belong quite yet."

Sarah will begin to feel comfortable in Geneva much faster if she can speak French passably well. If she has not had time to learn French before departure and if her husband's organization is not providing lessons, now is the time to sign on with one of the many language schools. She will no doubt find that her children outpace her in the language learning race.

Another way of lessening the blow of culture shock is to learn her way around as quickly as possible. She is fortunate to have an excellent guidebook, *Geneva for Beginners,* and an efficient and "user friendly" bus service. But a good map and sturdy walking shoes are her best aids to finding her way around in the early stages.

Let us suppose for a moment that Sarah does not have a career or that she wants time out for a few years to be a homemaker. What will she face? As we said earlier, her home

---

[5] Geneva Women's Cooperative, *With Our Consent?*

will probably be much smaller and require far less care, and she will not have a garden to occupy her. With extra time on her hands, she may want to develop friendships with similarly placed women, and one of the best ways of finding these women is through women's organizations. Even if she is not a joiner, attending a few meetings of such organizations just to meet people and see what is going on will be useful.

As we know, though, Sarah does want to pursue her career. Through contacts at her husband's firm she receives a job offer, but because Swiss law requires the employer to obtain a work permit for the spouse of someone already holding a permit, she has difficulties. It seems that in many cases employers are reluctant to go to the expense and effort of obtaining a work permit unless they are desperate for particular skills and cannot find them among the Swiss. A recent survey (conducted by Organization Resources Counselors, Europe, in association with the Confederation of British Industries Employee Relocation Council) confirms that the situation is problematic. One respondent is quoted as saying,

> "Most of our overseas assignments are to Switzerland [Geneva]. We have difficulty obtaining work permits for our own employees. To get one for the spouse would almost certainly be impossible."[6]

According to one woman in the GWC study,

> "The competition is tough here. In this city, no matter how good you are, if you don't know somebody on the inside, you're not going to get the job."[7]

---

6 Organization Resources Counselors, Europe, and Confederation of British Industries Employee Relocation Council, *Survey on Spouses/Partners and International Assignments,* vol. 2, London (19 January 1990). Summary of the findings and conclusions from the survey of company views and experiences.

7 Geneva Women's Cooperative, *With Our Consent?*

Unfortunately, therefore, it is difficult to be positive about the situation with regard to work for spouses, not just in Switzerland but in many European countries.

We now leave Sarah, not only coping with getting settled, shopping, finding schools for the children, learning the language and getting about, but also feeling great frustration at the thought of not being able to find work in her field. Clearly, it is an illusion for the British or others of European descent to think that adapting to a European assignment will be a simple matter just because it is in Europe. As for Sarah, we can only hope that through creativity and a large share of good luck, she will avoid having to say, as one European woman did to us,

> I will never again follow as a wife and mother. I've done enough of that before. Wherever we move next time must allow me to be rooted. I must have enough time . . . ten years perhaps. In other words, my husband's job will not be the primary consideration. I must be able to be professionally happy which means we must both be able to work.

ten

___

Moving Overseas with Children

Children can be likened to trees and flowers. Some thrive with uprooting, others wither and fade. There are times when it is good to move a plant; it all depends on its age and the season. The same is true for children.

All children, dependent or independent, preschool or high school, need special attention during the time of transplanting. They need nurturing and care from their parents throughout their time of adjustment. It is fatal to assume that "my child adjusts easily" or to think that children always land on their feet. They are not cats! They are people who have the same fears, anxieties, and excitement that their parents have about moving, though they may express them differently. There will be crankiness in one-year-olds, screaming tantrums in two-year-olds, defensiveness in the preteens, or outright rebellion in teenagers.

Most experts who study overseas children tend to consider the overseas experience a negative one. In contrast, Dr. Ruth Useem,[1] who has studied children overseas for more than thirty years, takes a more positive approach. She looks at the children, whom she calls "Third-Culture Kids," or TCKs, over the long term. She likens them to orchids, the rarest and most beautiful of flowers. When they bloom, their beauty has

___

[1] Dr. Ruth Useem (now retired) was a professor at Michigan State University who has studied overseas children as well as raised three of her own.

no equal; they carry their roots with them and need only be hung on a tree or put into a simple pot. But how right the climate must be for them to flourish! They need tender care and compatible conditions. When we raise orchids, as Nancy has, the rewards for our pains are reaped a hundredfold. The same holds true for children. As their parents, it is our job to provide an environment where they feel safe and secure and can develop their full potential.

There is no easy answer to the question, "How will children fare in a move overseas?" So much depends on them, their relationship with their parents, their situations, and the season of their lives. Some children meet each new experience with joy. They run down the path on the first day of school giving not so much as a backward glance to their mothers, who stand weepy on the doorstep. There are others, however, who move more slowly, each step a painful separation from the known. As these children embark on the unfamiliar, their whole being reflects their reluctance.

In between are all the other children, partly eager to move, partly desperate to cling, not unlike adults. But children have fewer ways of coping with the deep emotions that a move evokes. They may know that something is wrong, but cannot find words to express what it is. When that move is to a country where nothing is familiar, they feel a keen sense of loss which they cannot articulate.

Which children move the best? Infants move easily from place to place as long as they have the security of mother or father. However, toddlers, preschool children, preteens, and teenagers all need special consideration. Sidney Werkman, in his book *Bringing Up Children Overseas*, cautions against moving a child between the ages of seven and eleven.

Since the ages of seven to eleven are the time for the educational process to take hold, a child's school experience should be stable, serene and safe. It is unwise to overwhelm children with too many trips, disruption, or moves from house to house. When moves are necessary, they must be planned with great care.[2]

Teenagers are also difficult to move. They have a circle of friends and special needs and interests. We would suggest that you not move a child who is in a final year or two of high school. In order to make the right decisions, you need to know your children well. You must know what makes them happy or sad, brave or fearful; what gives them security or makes them feel insecure. Children whose parents have carefully considered their needs will have an easier adjustment than those whose parents make assumptions about their children which may not be true.

BEFORE DEPARTURE

Making the Decision

We once met with a group of teenagers to discuss living overseas and the stresses they experienced in a mobile lifestyle. For these young people, moving was a way of life. A quarter of them were veterans of four moves to four different countries. Another quarter were in their third country, and another quarter in their second. For only one quarter of the group was this their first move. Yet none of them knew why their parents chose to live overseas except to say: (1) their father was bored in his old job and wanted a change and (2) their father made more money overseas. These reasons were not satisfactory to them, nor should they be. Only one of the group said that his parents had discussed the move with him in any great detail, but he added ruefully, "I didn't have any power in that discussion."

---

[2] Sidney Werkman, *Bringing Up Children Overseas: A Guide for Families* (New York: Basic Books, 1977).

Like their adult counterparts, children need to be prepared for a move to a new country. Older children should know why they are going and what the move means for the father or mother's position. They need time to think about what it means to them. They need to know what the people in their new country will be like, how they will speak and act. They need time to say good-bye.

Children who have reached school age should be allowed to participate in the decision making. As they get older, the participation will be more sophisticated as their needs change. Parents must consider what their children lose, as well as what they can gain by a move. Share these ideas with the children. It might be a good idea to develop a balance sheet of pluses and minuses for a move, similar to the one parents develop for themselves. Remember, the parents' motivations for going and their perception of the children's needs may not be shared by the children.

You may think this move will be a great experience for your children, giving them a broader perspective and turning them into international citizens with a sensitivity to the wider world in which they live. But these are rather esoteric motivations and are rarely shared by the child, whose life revolves around his or her neighborhood and school. Parents must help their children to understand both the reasons for the move and the specific ways in which they can benefit from it themselves. Though children may appreciate the value of their father or mother getting a better job, it is not enough.

If the child has a valid reason for not wanting to go, like nearing the end of a high school career or studying for a college course that cannot be pursued overseas, some alternative may have to be found. Can the child board with friends or family until the schooling is completed? Is it possible for one parent to remain at home for a year? Some parents find that the needs of the teenager are so acute that leaving them behind is a viable alternative.

Preparation

Once the decision to go is made, the children should be included in as much of the preparation as possible. How much they can do will depend, of course, on their ages. Learning about a new country can be made into a game for the young ones by looking at books, studying the way people dress, learning some words of the language, and tracing on a map the route to be traveled. For older children, there may be an opportunity to explore their new experience with their classmates at school. Alert their teachers to the move and see if they will talk about the country of destination in history and geography classes. When children know that their friends and teachers are interested in where they are going, a positive note is added to this period of anticipation.

Another practical and positive approach to preparing for the move is to undertake some projects which include both the old and the new. Prepare a scrapbook or a family photo album to take with you, involving the children in the process. Help your children prepare an address book with their friends' names and addresses so they can maintain contact if they wish. The assurance that these links can be maintained is important, even if the children do not do so once overseas.

Saying Good-Bye

Take time to help the children say good-bye. Adults have learned that we rarely say good-bye to someone for the last time. Our past experience indicates that we will meet again, but our children do not have the benefit of that experience. They tend to feel that good-byes are forever. We need to give them the time and opportunity to say their good-byes and reassure them that they will see their friends and loved ones again. Here are some ways that can help:

- Give a farewell party for your older children's friends.
- Take the children to see family members, especially grandparents, who will promise to write and never for-

get the children. They will be a source of the love and
security the children need.

• Make that last trip to their favorite spot, be it the local
park or hamburger joint—even when there are several
"last trips."

Your children need to know that you too feel sad about
the separation from friends and loved ones. We cannot gloss
over the pain of saying good-bye, and we do our children a
disservice when we put on a brave face. It may look as if we
have no feelings at all. On one of Nancy's departures from her
parents' home in America, her father and mother did not accompany her to the airport, but waved good-bye as she and
her family drove off. The family waved back, crying openly
until the grandparents could no longer be seen. Five-year-old
Mike cried too. Later in the trip he said, "You really love
Grandpa and Grandmomma, don't you? I do too. I wish they
lived with us." How strange it would seem to the child if he
felt sad about leaving his grandparents, and his parents acted
as if nothing were wrong.

Packing

It is important that the children help choose the things
they would like to take with them. The favorite toy or book,
no matter how aged and weathered, will be much more comforting than the promise of something new. Some of the
things that you might have discarded, like the half-broken
truck or doll with the missing eye, will bring comfort when
everything else is new.

Involve the children as much as possible in the actual
packing—and the unpacking too. Though putting favorite
items in a shipping box may be traumatic at the time, the box
will eventually arrive overseas, and the expressions of delight
as familiar possessions are discovered will be worth the extra
hours it might take to pack and unpack with youngsters under-
foot.

Since the time prior to departure is usually frenetic, you may be tempted to leave the children with a friend or a sitter so that you can work more efficiently. Don't. A child who misses the packing day and comes home to see his room stripped of all his familiar things and his suitcase packed may experience a rather intense disorientation. Though it will mean more work, keep the children with you. You are their source of security during the move, and they need the close connection. If you need help with infants or toddlers, have someone come and keep an eye on them while you pack.

Orientation Programs

If your organization offers an orientation program for adults, ask if your teenagers may also attend. Orientation programs which include them can be valuable for the parents as well. The issues they raise may open new avenues of communication among family members. We recall one situation when a mother expressed her concerns about having so much material wealth when she lived overseas. She wondered aloud how she would feel being a "have" in a "have not" country. Her teenagers looked at her in amazement. They said that this question bothered them too, but they had thought their mother loved the idea of being rich. They gained a valuable insight into their mother's character and grew closer to her through the experience.

AFTER ARRIVAL

Getting About

Family outings are a good idea in the first weeks you are in a new post. Seek sites which will be fun for the children, like a zoo or amusement park. Introduce them to the local market, but slowly, and do not be surprised if their first reaction is negative. We have friends who wanted to introduce their children to everything, including the meat market, where all the animal parts were hung in the open at eye and nose level. For the entire three years they spent in that country, their children would eat no meat until assured that it was not from the market. These kids were not unusually fastidious, but they had grown up with supermarkets and meat neatly wrapped in plastic.

Too much exposure too soon is not recommended. But planned outings can be great fun, giving you the chance to discover and react to things together. Try to find places for weekend, day, or overnight trips which will take you away from where you live, particularly if it is a big city. Some countries abound with beautiful spots for weekend getaways; in others they are harder to find.

Helping the Children Adjust

While living overseas you have to spend more time managing your children's lives. A classic error is to expect too much too quickly from your child. Nancy recalls arriving at a new post and immediately placing her toddler in school. The tears began almost immediately. It turned out that though the teacher spoke and taught in English, the children were of mixed nationalities and spoke the local language when at play. Her child felt left out. Nancy's solution was to withdraw him from the school and allow him several months at home to adjust. She then enrolled him in a different school. The circumstances were the same, but by then he had adjusted to his surroundings and could cope with the language.

Adjustment can be particularly difficult for teenagers. They do not make friends as easily as younger children and are more inhibited in seeking parental help. They miss acutely what they have left behind and can be genuinely unhappy at first. Schools overseas tend to have high academic standards but often lack technical/vocational courses or competitive sports programs. The student who excels in these areas may be disappointed.

We recently met the parents of a sixteen-year-old boy

who is a talented runner. It was discouraging to learn that the school he was to attend had no organized track program and no physical education teacher who could coach track. Fortunately, he discovered that many adults in the community were competitive runners and participated in organized running events. They welcomed the boy. It may not have been the best of all worlds, but he could maintain his competitive edge and continue to participate in the sport he enjoyed.

Helping teenagers profit from their experiences abroad is a real challenge for parents. The school cannot meet all their needs, and opportunities for independence are limited. Teenagers will not be able to hold part-time jobs or work during holidays in order to earn their own money and gain experience outside the home, and they will probably not be allowed to drive a car. They will be dependent on you for simple things like pocket money and transportation. This dependence can make them resentful, especially when compared with the independence their peers at home enjoy, and they will not appreciate being told that life overseas gives them compensating opportunities to travel and explore exotic and unique places. Like all teenagers, those who grow up overseas want to be indistinguishable from other teenagers of their own nationality. The overseas experience may simply reinforce their feelings of being different and thus may not be welcome.

School and Related Concerns

Adjustment to school is another factor for parental concern. In large cities, schools are staffed by a combination of teachers imported from the United States and Europe and expatriates already living in the community who have teaching credentials. Normally, students have one teacher per subject for the entire year. But such is not always the case. In small communities or in schools which operate on small budgets, there is often total dependence on a staff of "local hire" teachers made up of expatriates and host nationals with teaching credentials. This situation makes for a less stable school environment, because teachers may leave in the middle of the year when their spouses are transferred. We have had friends whose children have had four and five teachers in one year, though this is unusual. In addition, whole subject areas may not be taught if qualified teachers cannot be found. It is best if the parents find out as much as possible about prospective schools prior to departure so that decisions can be made as to the advisability of bringing the children. If the school is not up to acceptable standards or is limited in its educational program, your child might be better served elsewhere.

For young children, a local school is an option, particularly for parents who feel that learning a second language and culture is important for their children. From age thirteen on, a child should attend a school which provides the necessary preparation for university or college.

Boarding schools are an option to consider. There are many good boarding schools which offer the children a stable environment while the parents move from country to country. Britons who live overseas commonly send their children home for schooling after the age of nine. Americans do not do so as frequently but it is an option which should not be ruled out. There may be good boarding schools in neighboring countries, necessitating fewer expensive trips back and forth.

In some countries the international school does not go beyond junior high school level (age twelve to thirteen) so that parents of senior high school students have to select from among several other options: a boarding school in a neighboring country, a boarding school in the home country, a school back home (where the student lives with friends or relatives), or correspondence courses. Boarding schools certainly have much more to offer a teenager than correspondence courses since the camaraderie of peers is important to them. Correspondence courses also need a highly skilled parent as surrogate teacher. Most of the children we have known who were sent to boarding school loved the experience, including the traveling back and forth. Parents are often not so happy, however. It is hard to let children go, especially when parents are so far away that close and regular communication is difficult. In a great fury of emotion, the child in school or university writes his or her parents with a problem. The distraught parents receive the letter, think out a response and call or write the student. At the same time, the parents usually check with the home support group. By the time all of this well-meaning concern reaches the student, the crisis has passed and he or she has a hard time remembering what the fuss is about.

Organizational and corporate employers vary in their willingness to pay for boarding schools and children's trips back and forth to post for visits. Check your organization's policies carefully so you are not taken by surprise should you decide on this option. Some will cover the costs of boarding schools only in your home country. Others will pay all school costs but only one holiday trip per year. This information should be available to you prior to your departure.

If you have a child with learning disabilities, there are few special classes in overseas schools. Even remedial reading and speech therapy are not always available. You may need to rely on your own resources and teaching skills or seek help in the community. Most larger expatriate communities have teachers who are interested in basic tutoring, but it is not as easy to find someone to work with a serious learning disability. Schools can be helpful, but do not rely on them.

You should bring educational materials and reference books along for all your children. Even for preschoolers, a supply of workbooks and writing tools is a good idea. In developing countries especially, good children's books are not available, so bring as many books as you can manage. If it turns out you do not need them, there will always be someone who does.

Hobbies and Other Activities

Materials for hobbies your children enjoy should be brought with you. Children will have more time than they did at home (partly because they will probably not be watching television). Plan so that they can spend this time on creative activities. It is too easy for a child to fall into a pattern of moping and being bored. Teenagers may tend to spend idle hours hanging around a club or similar place, being unproductive and often feeling very negative as a result.

Resources for the special interests or activities your child enjoys may not be available. If not, there are two things you can do: begin the activity yourself, or try channeling your child's interests in a new direction. If he or she has been an active scout and loves to hike or camp but no scouting program exists, look for another way to continue this activity. A child may like walking in the mountains or exploring coral reefs with a local group or alone. Develop new hobbies by directing your child to local resources that encourage, for example, the budding scientist or musician. Every country has its own special musical tradition, and opportunities to learn how to play instruments not common at home may exist. One young man came to Indonesia as a cello-playing teenager. While there he learned to play the gamelan, a Javanese/Balinese gong instrument. He is now an adult and still playing the gamelan, but with fellow Americans in the U.S.

Opportunities to improve skills in individual sports like swimming, tennis, or squash are often available to young people. Guide your children into activities which give them positive feelings both about themselves and about the country in which they are living.

Caretakers and Household Help

We have written about household help in general in Chapter 4. What do you need to know about their relationships with children?

There is value in having household help, but they should remain "help" and not become the main caretakers and nurturers of your children. That role should be filled by parents. You may find that having a caretaker (i.e., nursemaid) limits your own time with your child. If this is the case, there is no need to employ a nursemaid just because everyone else does. If you have more than one young child, a caretaker may be just what you want, since she will free you to be with one while she tends to the other(s). However, even in the latter case, remember that having a children's caretaker is a luxury to be enjoyed, not a perk to be abused to the detriment of your child.

Some children may resent being left with a caretaker. They may feel that their mother does not love them as much as she should because they are always being left behind. We have an adult friend who still harbors negative feelings about being raised by an *ayah* (a child's caretaker) in his early years. His mother was busy with a younger child, but no amount of intellectualizing about it allows him to overcome his sense of loss.

Werkman states the problem clearly:

> Both mothers and fathers need to budget a healthy block of their time if they expect to have psychologically healthy children. Overseas parents who retain the primary responsibility for their offspring will get love and trust from them in return. Conversely, parents whose young were cared for exclusively by outsiders will have children who feel rejected. No matter how much a "nanny" loves Johnny, that child will feel devalued because his parents were willing to give him to a caretaker. Underneath Johnny's anger will be his feeling that he was abandoned by parents who allowed him to be taken over entirely by someone else.[3]

We find that well-adjusted children overseas are most often the ones whose parents spend a lot of time with them. The quality and the quantity of the time are equally important. There has been much discussion in recent years about quality time with children. Working mothers have been assured that as long as the quality of the time they give to their children is

---

[3] Ibid.

high, the quantity is not important. We discussed this issue recently in a women's group without coming to a clear conclusion. Some weeks later we met one of the participants, a mother of an eighteen-month-old boy. She had just decided to turn her leave of absence into retirement from her job. She was joyous as she explained her decision to continue to be at home with her child. "I figured out that for me to get the quality, I have to put in the quantity."

Another young mother who has two preschool children and a full-time caretaker for them has become involved in many outside activities, leaving her children in the full care of this competent nursemaid for many hours each day and several nights in the week. When she returns home, she laments, she finds herself constantly in the role of teacher with little time left over simply to play with them. This is an unfortunate and even dangerous situation. If the nursemaids are having all the fun with your children and you become the harbinger of discipline and lessons each time you walk into the house, something is seriously wrong.

If you do hire a caretaker, careful selection is important. This person will be the single most influential member of your staff. You may want an unmarried girl who acts more like a playmate than a mother. Young women enjoy playing with children and can give them many hours of laughter and fun, similar to the role of the teenage babysitter at home. Or you may want to find someone who is older, who will mother and treat the child in the best traditions of the grandmother. Whichever you choose, be aware of the effect she will have on socializing your child.

One working mother has a two-year-old girl who spends a minimum of eight hours each day under the exclusive care of a nursemaid. This child is using the nursemaid as her role model. The mother comments that her daughter is very good at washing windows and scrubbing floors. Right now everyone thinks this is cute. But when does the mother have a chance to influence the child's development? By the time she comes home from the office, the child is ready for bed. The time for role modeling and transferring values is severely limited.

Children with absentee parents tend to be socialized into the caretaker's culture rather than that of the parents. Children who grow up in the exclusive care of nursemaids may have difficult adjustments to make when they return to their own culture. The relationships we need with our children are developed during the time we spend with them each day and cannot be established in a frantic "catch-up" effort just before or after returning home.

On the other hand, overseas living should not make us slaves to our children. We suggest that you allocate roughly the same time with them as you did at home. If you spent mornings at work or some other activity and your child was in a morning nursery or day care center, there is no reason to alter this pattern overseas. You may be substituting a nursemaid at home for the nursery school, but the idea will be the same, as will the time you spend with the child.

The problem of how the caretaker disciplines your child is a difficult one. Every culture has its own ways of disciplining children and they tend to vary substantially. In many cultures, children are frightened into submission. In former times, a Javanese villager would tell a naughty child that the "white men" or "Dutch priest" would come and take him away if he was bad. In other parts of Indonesia, children are told of a child-eating witch who comes after bad children at night or in weather which is a mixture of sun and rain. Stories of demons and spirits, ghosts and witches coming to get them can terrify young children. You have to protect them from these terrors by carefully monitoring your help.

Sometimes no discipline will be used at all; an angry or fretful child may be placated with sweets. This is generally not the way Westerners discipline children. The children quickly learn the parameters of the behavior their caretakers will accept, and the result is often undisciplined behavior by Western standards. In times of crisis and difficulty, caretakers will revert to their own cultural patterns and methods no matter what they have been told to do. No caretaker wants the mother to return home to a crying child; she fears for her job!

Nancy remembers Cairo and the nanny she had for her two-year-old son. As a mother of seven herself, she was a loving and unflappable lady and had the warm qualities Nancy looked for in her help. She spoke one word of English: "Bravo." Nancy had occasion to hear her use it when she returned home unexpectedly early one day. She was confronted with the sight of her son standing on the coffee table wildly throwing tennis balls at the chandelier. A direct hit and the inevitable tinkling of broken glass was accompanied by a huge smile, clapping of hands, and a hearty, "Bravo, Michael!" from Nadia, who could not understand Nancy's concern over her behavior or Michael's. "Boys may do as they wish," was her answer to this and any of his other antics. It was what her culture told her, but it was a value which diverged rather radically from Nancy's. In spite of Nancy's firm warnings about the game, it was clear that Michael was allowed to continue to play it.

Caretakers must be willing to do things the way you want them done, especially in the areas of hygiene and health. Not only do they need to be in good health themselves but they need to maintain a clean environment for the children. Many families have had unfortunate experiences with nurse-maids who thought there was nothing wrong in giving children sweet drinks from a street vendor or candies from a market stall. Not realizing the dangers to young stomachs, they have blithely allowed children to have whatever they craved. In one family, weeks of serious illness ensued, and it was some time before the anxious mother was able to trace the cause. If your caretaker persists in such practices after repeated instructions not to buy sweets off the street, the only course of action is to let her go rather than threaten your child's health.

Westerners tend to believe that children need space which belongs to them. When overseas, you may want to allow them to have their own rooms as havens and give your household help instructions not to go in and clean the room, no matter what it looks like. This will be as hard for the help as it is for you at times, but it is important if your child needs to have his or her own domain. Think of how you feel when the maid has cleaned your desk top and put everything away so that you cannot find anything. Your child will feel the same way when the Legos have been tidied up or the block house destroyed by a well-meaning maid who is trying to uphold your standards of household tidiness.

It is easy to raise lazy children when you have household help. Someone else will pick up the toys they leave scattered around the living room floor. They can throw off their dirty clothes and find them washed and ironed and in their drawer the next day. They can track mud into the living room with not so much as a backward glance at the maid madly hurrying to clean up after them. When you see these things happening, you will know that your child is not learning the basics of good manners and personal responsibility. It is important that you ask the same of your children as you would back home. They can clean their own rooms, help with clearing the dishes from the table after meals, care for their pets, or whatever is customary in your household. Always keep in mind that you are not likely to live overseas forever, and it is easier not to let patterns of laziness develop than to try and break them when you return home.

We watched one friend frantically try to make up for several years of neglected training. Her young children had had a maid to take care of all their needs during their early years. When she and her husband decided to return home, they realized they were in for a drastic change in family life-style. The children would have to learn to care for themselves. The retraining was an arduous process for the parents, the children, and the household help as the mother tried to change her children's behavior patterns three months prior to departure. She forced the children to pick up their clothes and toys, clean their rooms, and dress and feed themselves. She began each day with a "when we get back to America" lecture, so upsetting the children that they began to resent the idea of going to this "America place" and fought tooth and nail against her short course in disciplined habits. The mother ruefully admitted that it would have been much easier to have prevented them from becoming so lazy in the first place. Playing "catch-up" with your children's habits is not fair to them or to you.

Clear guidelines on how children and staff should behave toward each other must be established from the beginning. Servants are adults and should be accorded the same respect that any adult in the child's life receives. When children behave rudely to the help, they need to be corrected. Most help dislike denying children any request, no matter how rudely demanded or how absurd, because they fear displeasing them. So you need to monitor child/staff relationships closely until your own values are firmly established and understood by both. If not, you may find your children stuffed with candy and ice cream just before dinner and fast becoming accomplished tyrants.

Scheduling Your Social Activities

Children like routine and need to know that their parents will be with them and perform certain functions at certain times. If you yield, for instance, to the temptation of going out every night, which is easy to do in most countries overseas, your children will suffer no matter what their age or the competency of their caretaker. Young children miss their usual bedtime routines and will feel insecure in their new house without their parents to "protect" them. Nancy's child was fluent in the local language and would play happily with the staff during the day. But at night the caretaker could not read to him, so he fought against his parents going out. To ease the situation, they limited their nights out and hired an American teenager to sit on evenings when they did go out.

People whose professional positions include obligatory social functions are wise to set rules for their social calendar.

We know one successful businessman who never goes out two nights running or more than three nights in a week. His children can depend on this schedule and understand when their parents must attend a social function.

Living with New Social Customs

Even though the lives of school-age children revolve around the school, they still need to know how to get along in the broader cultural environment. Teenagers will be most affected and influenced by the place where they live since they are the most mobile. They will want to go to public places on their own and, in order to be comfortable, must learn how to behave appropriately according to local customs.

Behavior and dress which are appropriate at home may be offensive in the new country. It is the rare American girl, for example, who dresses with the decorum adhered to by her counterpart in an Asian or Middle Eastern country. Halter tops and short shorts have been accepted in the West for some time. Not so in Asia and the Middle East. If a teenager appears in such attire in New Delhi or Dubai, she can easily become the target of rude or even frightening behavior.

Other differences in customary behavior are much more subtle and deserve careful attention. "When in Rome, do as the Romans do" is an excellent rule of thumb. It is the responsibility of the parents to help their children adjust, even if it means clipping their wings a little at first.

Teenagers tend quickly to retreat from the culture if their first experiences are unpleasant. They need to know the rules to ease their transition.

Drink, Drugs, and Sex

Many parents believe they will leave some of the more difficult social problems of teenagers behind when they move overseas. Not true! Drink, drugs, and sex are as much a part of life in Sydney, Bangkok, and Istanbul as they are in Washington, Mannheim, or Keokuk. In some ways the problems become even greater overseas where there is less for teenagers to do to occupy their time.

In some countries drugs are very accessible; in others alcohol is simple to obtain because there is no enforced age restriction on the purchase of alcohol. Imagine the absolute disbelief of one set of parents who on their first weekend overseas allowed their fourteen-year-old daughter to attend a party with children her own age at the home of an office colleague, only to discover that not only was there free and open drinking, but the chief bartender was the father of the house.

These problems are exacerbated by the fact that there are fewer places for teenagers to go for information or to obtain help in clarifying their values. No Planned Parenthood clinics cater to the needs of teenagers; few programs on drug and alcohol abuse exist. Teenagers need guidance from their parents because they will not have other positive community supports or helping agencies to lean on. And there will be plenty of negative influences and much social pressure to join the gang.

In some overseas communities, parents have joined together with the help of local experts to develop programs on these social issues. Such programs can be effective, giving the teenagers a larger reference group and more role models to imitate, but they do not negate parental responsibility. Your children need to know where you stand on these issues and be able to talk to you about the problems they are facing.

Keeping Your Own Culture Alive

It can come as a shattering surprise to discover that your young children know little or nothing about their own country. This is particularly true of children who were born overseas and have been home only for short leaves. We think of them as American or British or German, but do *they*? While attending a ceremony at the U.S. ambassador's residence which was opened by a Marine color guard and the reciting of the pledge of allegiance to the flag, Nancy suddenly realized that her five-year-old son did not know what was going on. Another mother standing nearby was having the same astonished reaction to her young daughter. Both children had been born overseas and did not know some of the basic customs of their countries, customs which their parents took for granted.

It is important for children to have roots, to know their own culture and feel proud of it. When they return to that culture, as they are virtually certain to do at some stage in life, it will be much more difficult if they are completely out of step with its customs and traditions. Many families overseas make a conscious effort to instill a sense of tradition in their children. Barbara once travelled in India with several families, one of whom was American. These Americans had been overseas for some time but still celebrated Thanksgiving every year as though they were back in their native Maine. It so happened that Thanksgiving fell during a train journey that year but they were undaunted. The carriage had been pulled over to a siding in the town they were visiting and you can imagine the amazement of the local population when the cook set up an oven on the station platform and proceeded to prepare Thanksgiving dinner, complete with turkey, mashed potatoes and cranberry sauce, followed by pumpkin pie! It was served in style, buffet fashion, on the seat of the train carriage and Barbara never had a better Thanksgiving dinner. This may seem a bit extreme to you and have overtones of the British gentleman in the jungle dressing for dinner every night. But the British did it for a reason and so should we. It was a conscious effort to maintain the health of their own cultural roots no matter where they lived in the world because someday they would be returning home.

Girls and the Role-Model Gap

We were once involved in a Girl Scout program on career opportunities for women which provided some dramatic insights into the problems girls (and their mothers) face overseas.

The scouts were asked what their mothers did. The answers were brutally honest.

> "My mother cries a lot."
> "My mother gets mad."
> "Mine takes care of my brother."
> "My mother does nothing."

Not one of the twenty or so girls saw her mother's role as a positive one, and only one said she wished to be like her mother. The final comment came when the "actress" in the group jumped to center stage and said: "This is my mother talking to my father." Placing her hands on her hips she started shouting, "I wish we'd never come here. If we were home, I'd have my job and things wouldn't be like this!" Dropping the angry pose, the little girl said, "And this is my dad." She folded her arms across her chest and spoke in a very slow, low voice: "But, we agreed this would be a good change for all of us and that it would be fun." The little girl flopped into her place with one final comment: "The trouble is, for my mom, this place isn't any fun."

For many of these girls, their mothers project such an unhappy and victimized image that the girls themselves feel limited in what they will be able to do with their lives. Most women overseas do not have the kind of job and status they could or would have in their home country. For a variety of usually very understandable reasons, they have given up their own careers or put them aside. Yet in doing so, the image they project to their daughters is one of unhappiness and lack of self-esteem. In addition, there are fewer positive role models for girls in most countries overseas than at home. They are not seeing successful aunts, grandmothers, or neighborhood women who do different things. Their school teachers provide good models but there are few others. They are unlikely to be exposed to women in business or who hold other responsible positions. As a result, the role their mother projects becomes much more important. We believe that what mothers actually *do* overseas is not so important to their daughters as how they feel about it. If the mother is out of control, and shows it, the young girl does not have much to emulate. You can hardly convince a girl that she can be whatever she sets her mind to if you are doing nothing that indicates you are that kind of woman. Girls need to understand that their mothers may have given up something to come overseas and should be told what the trade-offs were. What did she give up and what has she gained because of the move?

Surrogate Families

In every foreign community there are willing "grandparents" as well as a host of "uncles" and "aunts" who can take great pleasure in your child's life. Sharing holidays and other family events with them gives you a sense of having an extended family and fills an important need for them as well. Adopted relatives of this kind can provide a continuity and sense of security for children that their natural uncles and aunts, because of distance, cannot. They often become lifelong friends who keep in touch long after the children have moved to another part of the world.

It is also important to maintain relationships with relatives at home. Nancy's son maintains a thriving correspondence with one of his grandmothers. She sends regular letters and pictures which he answers with school drawings and other things he creates. He sends tapes which he records privately. He looks forward eagerly to the time when he can go home alone for the summer and spend time with his grandparents because he feels he knows them so well.

International Citizens

How often we have heard, "Our children will become international citizens and develop a sensitivity to other cultures and people because of living overseas." This happens, but not necessarily while they are actually living abroad. Many years later they may look back on the experience as one of personal growth, but it takes time for them to appreciate what they have gained. Many parents worry that their children want to be involved only with school activities or with other expatriate children and rebel when they are required to visit the local temple or museum. Try to accept these reactions. Expose them to what they can tolerate and help them learn what they can from the experiences, but do not force them. International citizens are not created by requiring children to sit through cultural performances which they neither like nor wish to understand. A friend of ours has become an international citizen in part because he grew up overseas. Yet, because he was overexposed as a child, he will not go to a museum or other "place of interest" without great prodding. He despised it then and he despises it now!

Ruth Useem's research indicates that 80 percent of the children who grow up overseas work as adults in an international field—for international agencies or multinational corporations in an overseas setting, or as teachers of foreign languages and cultures or other international subjects at home. They will almost inevitably have a broad worldview. It helps if the parents can take a long-range perspective and relax. Let the children enjoy and absorb whatever they can according to their ages and personalities.

When to Seek Outside Help

With their parents' help, children usually adjust well to living overseas and look back on the experience as a valuable one. But sometimes children require more assistance than parents can give and may benefit from professional guidance. Do not be afraid to seek counselling for your children (or for the family as a whole) if the problems are beyond your capabilities to solve. Many expatriate communities and international schools have counsellors available who are familiar with the adjustment problems of children who are raised overseas. Availing yourself of this type of help does not indicate parental failure, but rather demonstrates your concern and your understanding that the child needs something different from what you are able to offer.

eleven
___
Staying Healthy Overseas

Moving anyplace where medicine is practiced differently than at home is likely to cause concern about the quality and the cost of health care. Family members may worry about differences in treatment, the prospect of entrusting their health to strangers, difficulties in establishing rapport with medical personnel (language problems in dealing with health issues can be particularly frustrating), or the basic health standards that are practiced in the country. Such questions arise as: How can I stay healthy? What if I get sick? What foods are available to make up a good diet? Are foods safe? How can I keep my children healthy?

Health care may not be perfect in your own country but you understand the procedures and the system. When ill, everyone needs familiar routines in order to feel that they are getting good treatment.

Sending organizations sometimes overdramatize health dangers, particularly when preparing personnel bound for developing countries. They err on the side of caution, particularly in describing the poor health standards that may exist in a country. When you hear statistics on infant and child mortality and are told about the prevalence of disease, it is important to remember that these figures are for the host country population. Because developing countries do tend to have large segments of the population suffering from poor nutrition and living in substandard health conditions, many diseases are endemic, and the figures on morbidity and mortality are alarming. But expatriates rarely live under those conditions; the figures, therefore, do not mean the same to them as they do to the host country population.

Nevertheless, when you move you should be aware of the health problems that do exist and familiarize yourself with their causes and symptoms, the precautions you can take against them, and their treatment. Keep in mind that most of these problems will never affect you because you will be able to control your living conditions. If you find yourself in a potentially unhealthy situation, such as using public latrines or having access only to contaminated water supplies, you will be able to take corrective steps.

Concerns about health can become so overpowering that some people find themselves unable to think of anything else. They spend all their time reading health manuals and worrying about every symptom, fearing that it is the precursor of a frightening and dangerous disease. In this chapter, we present our perspective on staying healthy overseas. Our comments are based on our own experience, as well as that of other long-term overseas residents, and from medical practitioners who work abroad.

It is good to remember that you can maintain a healthy environment for your family most of the time. If someone becomes ill, you can handle it. The main thing you need to do is keep your head and follow the basic, sound health principles which you would use anywhere in the world.

MEDICAL CARE IN THE NEW COUNTRY

As soon as possible after arrival seek a doctor who can meet your family's needs. Find out what to do in an emergency, such as an accident or heart attack. What procedures should be followed, for instance, if you are involved in a traffic accident?

If you feel that you are not receiving the advice and treatment you would like when you are ill, seek a second opinion. In most overseas communities there are expatriate medical personnel who, while not working in clinical medicine, are willing to be consulted when a fellow expatriate is sick. Though it is unfair to consult them for free medical advice at every social occasion, they are usually willing to help when an illness does not seem to be responding to treatment by a local doctor.

The Home Medicine Chest

It is good to take a basic selection of medicines and medical supplies with you to your new home. While you will be able to purchase some of them locally, others may be unavailable. If you pack an initial supply, you will not need to worry about how to find them during those first few difficult weeks.

A fever is one of the first signs of infection. Have a reliable thermometer in your home medicine chest and be sure to include a rectal thermometer if you have young children. Fever strips can be useful though they are not totally accurate. After you have treated the fever, monitor progress and wait for further symptoms to develop.

A few books should also be included in your medical cupboard. At the head of the list is a good manual on health care. A first aid manual is also useful. For women of childbearing age, books on pregnancy, breast feeding and the care of the newborn are helpful, especially if you are going to a developing country where such books are not generally available. You may want to add a book on drugs and their side effects, written for laypeople, to your overseas library. For those of you going to remote areas, Werner's *Where There Is No Doctor* may be of use.[1]

If you will be traveling in the more remote areas of a country or across national borders in the developing world,

---

[1] David Werner, *Where There Is No Doctor: A Village Health Care Handbook* (Palo Alto: The Hesperian Foundation, 1977).

carry disposable syringes for injections in case they are needed. Otherwise you risk getting hepatitis, AIDS, or a myriad of other diseases from contaminated needles. Keep in mind that there is also risk of infections from transfusions as blood can be contaminated. Barbara was glad she followed this advice when she was sent to the airport of a large Asian city to get yellow fever injections prior to a trip to Africa. The attendant took a rusty tray out of a drawer, on which were two or three syringes which had obviously been used frequently without any cleaning at all. The man was quite happy to use her disposable syringes, which, she suspects joined the others on the tray.

HEALTH ISSUES IN DEVELOPING COUNTRIES

The following points apply mainly to those who will be working in developing countries where health standards are not as favorable as those in the West and where the prevalence of diseases of all types can be high. It is possible to stay healthy if your family follows the guidelines suggested here.

Cleanliness and Pest Control

If you are living in a developing country, you will probably have to work hard to maintain a home which meets basic Western health standards. In tropical countries where the environment and climate are often relatively unhealthy, household cleanliness is very important. Homes should be well lit and ventilated and have screened windows. Fans or air conditioning are important in warm, humid countries where fungus can grow overnight. You find that your shoes, beautiful one day, are covered with a grey-green, hairy slime the next. To control the humidity, many people use a dehumidifier. Even a light bulb kept on in the clothes cupboard can help.

Where there are many types of insect pests such as cockroaches, termites, ants, and flies (as well as rats and mice), routine spraying of grounds and the interior of houses is warranted. Follow the example of long-term residents. Vigilant pest control is necessary since you may be the only household in the neighborhood doing it. The invasion of pests from the outside is continuous, so that a routine prevention program is necessary. It is never enough to do this sort of thing once. Barbara once had a cook who had a deadly aim with a slingshot and occupied his off-duty hours shooting rats around her perimeter fence, contributing in great measure to her eradication program.

Health of Household Help

If you have household help, money invested in routine health care for them will pay dividends. Prior to employment, send them for a physical examination which includes blood, urine, and stool testing. These are done to check for communicable diseases, both venereal and parasitic. In countries where tuberculosis is endemic, every member of your staff should have a yearly chest x-ray or skin test.

When a member of your staff becomes ill, medical care should be provided promptly and you should supervise the administration of any medication prescribed. Why? In some countries, medication is feared. In others, the people believe so absolutely in the power of medicine that they feel "more is better" and take the whole bottle at one time. There are also cultural factors which affect the use of medicine. It is best, therefore, if the employer takes charge and sees that medication is used as directed, especially if it is "Western" medicine.

There may be traditional healers and traditional medicines used locally for which your staff has a preference. It may be difficult for you to appreciate this preference, but it is best to let your staff use the type of health facility with which they are most comfortable.

A case in point is Nancy's night watchman who developed a cough. It was probably caused by working outside all night during the rainy season. He went to the doctor and received some cough medicine. As he was coming home from the doctor, he fell or was pushed off the bus and developed leg troubles. To Nancy these were two unrelated problems, but her night watchman interpreted them differently, believing that someone or something was trying to do him harm. To recover he would need to go to his home village and visit a certain healer who made a special herbal drink. No amount of care from the doctor would cure him. Finally, he went off to the village and two weeks later returned in budding good health. What cured him? One cannot be sure, but he was convinced that it was the special medicine of the traditional healer.

It is important to allow people to use their own healing methods since they are part of the culture and may have psychological as well as physiological value to those who are members of it. However, it is a good idea to establish how much you are willing to pay. Traditional, just like modern medicine, has its share of charlatans ready to charge all the market will bear.

Household Help and Hygiene

Hygiene in the home is important anywhere, but in most developing countries it must be strictly observed. In your own country, you can probably be quite lax about leaving dust and tracked mud around for a Saturday morning scrub-down. This is not a problem because the air and water are not contaminated with fecal dust and other harmful pollutants as they are in some countries.

Household help must routinely wash their hands before handling food (especially after using the toilet) and clean their fingernails. They should be provided with clean and appropriate toilet facilities, a bathing area which fits their cultural standard and, if they live in your house, appropriate sleeping and eating facilities free of pests. They may also need to be taught not to leave food uncovered.

To encourage these practices, many employers provide articles for personal hygiene (soap, towels, toothpaste, tooth brushes, and nail brushes), as well as clothing to wear for work. This is a good idea and costs you little. Other employers provide food or food money so that their staff will eat a balanced diet.

Nancy had a houseboy who could not throw anything away. When she checked his room she would find old tins, crumpled newspapers, dry ballpoint pens, broken toys, and bits of old rags. He insisted that he might find a use for them someday. His room was a fire trap and an open invitation to pests. Since he could not part with his junk, Nancy eventually had to part with him. Staff quarters are really a part of your house, so it is not practical to allow unsanitary conditions to go unchecked. It is appropriate routinely to inspect the staff quarters to insure that they are properly maintained.

You will also probably encounter variations in the way cultures define behaviors as hygienic and unhygienic. Practices which Westerners consider impolite and unhygienic, such as spitting or picking feet, may be routine among the household help. On the other hand, you will find in many cultures that the practice of keeping dirty handkerchiefs in one's pocket and of sitting in dirty water while bathing are abhorrent. If you want your cultural standards met, you may need to provide constant reminders.

If there are young children in the household, special care must be taken in the preparation of their food. Babies who are bottle-fed will be vulnerable to infection, and mothers have to carefully supervise sterilization procedures. One of the reasons breast feeding is strongly recommended for all babies in developing countries is that it is difficult to assure that clean water is available and used for sterilization.

Babies and toddlers are oral beings who constantly put things into their mouths. They need to be watched carefully. If the tap water is contaminated, medical personnel may recommend boiling baby's bath water. It is easier to boil the bath water than to turn bath time into a nightmare of trying to keep water, toys and washcloths out of baby's mouth.

Water and Food Preparation

Contaminated water can be the source of a variety of infections and diseases such as cholera, typhoid, hepatitis, and parasitic diseases. Care must be taken in the boiling, filtering, and storage of water. In some places only boiling is necessary. In others, boiling and filtering are essential. Filtering is done to remove mineral particles such as mica (prevalent in Nepal, for instance). Check with long-term residents to find out what is required. Be sure your household help understand the process. Many understand about boiling water but then put it into a dirty filter or dirty storage bottles.

Give the help a kitchen timer to use while boiling water. Without a timer, water may be brought to a boil only, or bubble to nothing for an hour, depending on the perception of how long twenty minutes is. In the first case you risk becoming ill, in the second you are wasting fuel.

In hot countries where you will want a good supply of cold drinking water, boiled water may be kept in the refrigerator in used liquor bottles which have been cleaned and sterilized. When you're first setting up house, see if someone can lend you a few. Remember to make your ice from boiled water too.

Children must be constantly cautioned not to drink water from the tap. Use boiled water when making anything that will not be boiled for twenty minutes in the cooking process, for example, coffee and tea, condensed soups, gravies, cake mixes, and pie crusts. Use it as well for cooking vegetables, especially if you like your vegetables crisp.

Brush your teeth with boiled water. The bottle of boiled water on the bathroom counter is a standard item where there is a contaminated water supply. If you find yourself in a situation where boiled water is not easily available or you are unsure about it (some hotels in provincial areas, for example), the next best thing to use is bottled soda water. You get a delightfully effervescent effect when brushing your teeth! To quench your thirst when you are out, a bottle of soda drunk through a straw is the safest solution.

Fruits and vegetables may be grown in fecal-contaminated soil or watered with contaminated water and must be chemically treated before eating. Solutions of iodine, potassium permanganate, or bleach (Milton or Clorox) can be used for soaking. Check with others in the community about local practice. Remember to rinse the food with boiled water after soaking. Any fruit or vegetable that can be peeled should be. Children must be cautioned over and over never to eat any fruits or vegetables with the skins on unless it comes from their own kitchen.

In general, it is unwise to eat any raw fish, shellfish, or eggs. Meats should be well-cooked before consumption. Dairy products can be a problem. Fresh milk and cream will usually have to be boiled. It is best to check on local dairy products before using them. You may be better off using powdered milk in some places. Few countries in the developing world have adequate cold storage facilities. Even though food may be prepared in the cleanest of surroundings, spoilage and contamination are possible en route to the consumer.

Food stalls by the side of the road are a common sight, and the smells tempt the palate as you pass by. Some of them are safe and some are havens for disease. Check with expatriates in the community about eating in these stalls. Introduce your digestive system slowly to the new tastes and spices. It is wise to be cautious. Your system will be adjusting to many new things, stress will be high, and your body's ability to fight germs will be lower when you first arrive. Your stomach will protest if you try all ten of those lovely new tropical fruits in one day. You do have time, so take it easy.

It is the rare family whose members do not pick up a simple traveler's diarrhea in the early days of life in a new country. It can be caused as easily by stress and nervous tension as by a change in food and water. Be prepared to treat it with bland foods, lots of liquids to avoid dehydration, and rest. It should clear up quite naturally in a few days. Simple diarrhea does not require medication and, in fact, medications can be harmful. If the diarrhea persists or if there is severe cramping and a fever, seek medical help.

THE COMMON-SENSE APPROACH TO HEALTH

Three areas of health maintenance are important—rest, proper nutrition, and exercise and recreation. That is not telling you anything new; you know a healthy body requires them. But many people who live overseas ignore these basic rules of good health.

Rest

Consider rest and sleep. There is no doubt that when in hot climates or in stressful jobs, or with crammed social calendars, there is a tendency to forget the importance of a good night's rest. The amount of rest you need at home simply may not be enough when living abroad where there are often different and more stresses on the mind and body. Try to follow the rule of seven or eight hours of sleep each night. When you deny your body the rest it craves, you limit your ability to perform well and to cope with new situations.

For children, the need for extra rest and an early-to-bed schedule is quickly apparent, especially in a hot climate. Children who may have stopped taking an afternoon nap at home may need to have it reinstated, though it can probably be dropped again once their bodies have acclimatized.

Many people living overseas adopt the daily schedule of their hosts. In tropical countries people rise early and work hard in the coolest part of the day, rest during the hot midday, and rise again to continue activities in the relatively cooler evening. Some expats receive no visitors or phone calls between the hours of two to four in the afternoon. They may not be napping but they are certainly in an air-conditioned bedroom with their feet up.

Nutrition

Proper nutrition is something many adults think is important for children but not for themselves. In fact, adults too need a balanced diet for good health. Social life overseas can tempt you to eat too much snack food and consume too many calories in alcohol. Over a period of time, your body is going to react adversely to this ill treatment.

Whoever is cooking for the family must know the basic rules of good nutrition. Plan meals with the cook at first. Watch the cooking process so nutrients are not lost from excessive boiling. The cook may like to prepare the vegetables early in the day and leave them soaking in water until dinner time when they are cooked. Do not allow it.

In some countries, the soil is lacking in essential minerals and nutrients. When combined with a short tropical growing season, the result may be that food does not have all the nutriment you expect. Many people add a vitamin/mineral supplement (some add several different vitamins) to make up for the lack. Vitamins are not harmful when taken in moderation, but try not to overdo it. In some cases, as with Vitamin A, more is not better. Certainly, if you or your children are constantly ill, you should see it as a warning sign that your bodies may not be getting enough disease-preventive nutrients.

Forcing children to eat what you think they should is generally not advisable. It is often better to let them eat what they want, just so you make sure they get enough of whatever it is. One small boy wanted nothing but raw vegetables and ice cream during his first summer in a hot country. The mother was worried, but was assured by her nutritionist husband that the child would thrive if sufficient quantities of the foods he liked were available. There were and he did. This may be a reasonable approach to adopt. But if your child wants only soft drinks, candy, and potato chips, you will probably want to spend some time finding suitable alternatives.

Exercise and Recreation

Exercise and recreation promote good health in any environment, and being overseas is no exception. Look for opportunities to participate in sports. They abound in most countries. Squash, tennis, swimming, jogging, and walking are the most common. Sports facilities are often maintained by embassies and organizations for the use of their employees. In the larger cities, many hotels open their recreational facilities to local residents for a fee. Some of these are very good and offer a bonus, the chance to meet people you might not otherwise encounter. Many women join or start exercise clubs. As long as you exercise regularly, almost any form will do.

SAFETY AND THE PREVENTION OF ACCIDENTS

Most accidents occur in the home and are easily preventable. There are three main areas of concern when living overseas: electricity, fire, and the use of machines by household help.

Electricity

Most countries outside of the United States run on a current of 220–240 volts; U.S. current is 110 volts. If one is unfortunate enough to get a shock from 220 current, it can be incapacitating or deadly. Often, electricity is not well grounded (in some places not at all) and thus the dangers of using electricity increase.

We recommend that you cover all electrical sockets when they are not in use, even if there are no children in the house. Hide cables as much as possible. More than one pet has been killed by biting through a cable and many a maid shocked while washing the floor. Try to ground all appliances. If this is not possible or you are not sure that they are grounded, be sure that you and your help wear shoes and have dry hands when using appliances. Many of the people you hire will not have electricity in their own homes and certainly will not have appliances. They will be unaware of the dangers. Barbara had a maid in Nepal who frequently got a shock when she touched the refrigerator, though it never happened to Barbara. She finally realized that the maid did not wear shoes in the house and often had wet feet and hands.

Power failures occur regularly in many developing countries. While not necessarily a safety hazard, they can be devastating to your appliances. The power returns with a great surge and the damage to sensitive electrical equipment can be irreparable. Be sure to turn audio equipment, air conditioners, and even refrigerators off during power failures. You may want to connect your sensitive equipment to voltage regulators to prevent power surge damage.

Fire

If you face power failures, you will want to keep a supply of candles or kerosene lamps, both of which are potential fire hazards and should be kept in safe places and used with care.

Keep fire extinguishers handy and maintained ready for use, and make sure you and your staff know how to use them. You may also want to consider installing smoke detectors—if so, take them with you.

Use of Machines by the Household Help

Appliances such as mixers, blenders, and toasters become such a part of modern life that it is easy to forget that household help may be using them for the first time. Give them careful instructions. It is not unusual for an untrained cook to try to stop an electric mixer by putting his hand in the bowl and grabbing the beaters. Respect their wishes if they indicate they would prefer to do something the hard way rather than use one of your labor-saving devices. You might even find that you prefer soup pushed through a sieve to that made in a blender.

OTHER HEALTH FACTORS

Local Health Situation

Know the common diseases or health risks endemic to the area to which you are moving.Is it a malarial area? If so, find out what malaria prophylactic is recommended (they change from area to area as resistance to a particular prophylactic develops). Other common diseases may include tetanus, typhoid fever, whooping cough, and hepatitis, for each of which there are vaccines available. Children should have their routine immunizations up to date as well as those for mumps, measles, and rubella. Consult a physician for current information about the specific shots recommended for the area to which you are going.

Recovery Time

In tropical countries, it may take longer to recover from sickness than in temperate climates. It is not easy to break the cycle of illness, and more rest, in particular, may be required. At home it is probably common practice to allow children to resume their normal activities after twenty-four hours of being free from fever. This practice is usually not advisable in the tropics. Children recover more slowly, especially from serious dysentery. Medicines used for treating dysentery kill the organisms which cause the illness, but they also kill the beneficial organisms which live in healthy intestinal tracts. It is common for a child to recover from one bout of dysentery only to be struck down by another a few weeks later. The only way to break this cycle is to keep the child in a protected environment, encourage the intake of body-building foods and vitamins, and then slowly reintroduce him to his regular routine.

If illness strikes often, it is time to recheck the household help. Be sure that they are following the hygiene routines that you laid down. It may be that your child has become ill in his own home because of their carelessness.

Health Problems with Pets

Pets can be a health hazard, either because they have their own illnesses or because they may pass illnesses on to your children when they are infested with worms, ticks, fleas, or mange (which are common among animals in tropical countries). Pets should be checked regularly for these problems and corrective measures taken immediately. Also, see to it yourself; do not leave the health care of the animals to the staff.

Exotic or interesting domesticated pets are often available overseas: monkeys, apes, birds of all kinds, and various marsupials. If you want one, buy it from a reputable place which offers some assurance that it is disease-free. This is a tall order, since most animals are unceremoniously plucked from their native habitat (often by killing the mother) and taken posthaste to the pet market.

If you do decide to have pets, find a competent veterinarian who can check all the animals when you acquire them.

Rabies is still endemic in many parts of the world and, if contracted, is always fatal. Make sure the pets you acquire are, or have been, inoculated. If someone is bitten and the animal cannot be captured or confined, it is essential to assume the worst and proceed with rabies immunization.

Don't Panic

A psychologist who works with people living overseas says that the fear people most often express is fear of getting sick. Parents can become very alarmed when their child develops a fever, especially in countries where typhoid, cholera, and/or malaria are present. They tend to assume the worst rather than treating the fever matter-of-factly (as they would at home) until other symptoms develop. Many are amazed to discover that after frantically consulting medical manuals and bathing the fevered brow, the child gets up in the morning with a cold and a runny nose.

Of course, there are frightening moments when someone gets a more serious disease or a virus of undetermined nature, but that is the exception rather than the rule. There are few diseases that cannot be treated by modern medicine if tended to promptly.

Health horror stories abound in all overseas posts. Old-timers take delight in filling the newcomers in on all the worst. Even the best-prepared newcomer may have trouble maintaining a balanced perspective when the horror stories are compelling. When you hear a story, ask these questions: Is it a common occurrence or did it happen only once? Could it have been avoided through health precautions? Is it something which really could happen? Are you hearing about it firsthand or has the story come down through a variety of sources?

You may find it difficult to sift the data. You cannot shut your ears to all you hear. The best thing you can do is keep your head. If you are genuinely worried about a health problem in your new country, find out as much about it as you can. Learn from competent people, not your next door neighbor who heard it from her friend who heard it from the Smiths' childminder.

twelve

Reentry

The word *reentry* became part of our vocabulary with the advent of space exploration and the return of the capsule or vehicle into Earth's atmosphere. It was a traumatic experience, both for the capsules and for the people they carried.

A more recent meaning of *reentry*, the return to one's own culture after living in another, is the subject of this chapter. This experience can be just as traumatic as the return of a spacecraft to Earth. Why? "Who says we can't go home and feel good about it?" ask returning sojourners, occasionally with a hint of belligerence. "Going home completes the cycle of our travels and should be a happy experience." For many, this is not the case.

We will examine the process of reentry and suggest ways to ease the impact. The process is really an additional step in cross-cultural adjustment, occasionally referred to as *reverse culture shock*. Most sojourners find that reentry has as many, if not more, pitfalls than the move abroad, particularly if it is not well thought through. We share the opinion of many who have done research on the subject that people experience difficulty in reentry because they do not prepare themselves for going home with the same meticulous care they used in preparing for going abroad. Thus, when they unexpectedly find that life at home is not as they imagined it, the ensuing depression and discouragement are harder to live with than they were in the new culture.

As stated in *Helping Them Home,* by Margaret Pusch and Nessa Loewenthal,

... reentry for many, possibly most, sojourners never really ends in the sense that they are unable to become part of the home culture in a way that they were before departing. They may and often do continue searching for ways to extend or re-create the overseas experience and/or ways to use the competencies they have acquired by living in another country or culture, possibly with little success.[1]

So, whether or it is intended or not, living in another culture continues to influence most sojourners' lives long after the return home.

PREPARING FOR THE RETURN

As inveterate list makers, we recommend that you begin your preparations for returning home by making one. It should include the things you need to think about.

1. Why are you leaving?
2. How have you changed?
3. How has home changed?
4. What are the stages of reverse culture shock and what effect do they have?
5. Where will you settle?
6. What do you face if you return to work?
7. What must be done for the children?
8. How will your finances be affected?
9. What records will you need?
10. What do you most want to do when you get home?

---

[1] Margaret Pusch and Nessa Loewenthal, *Helping Them Home: A Guide for Leaders of Professional Integration and Reentry Workshops* (Washington, DC: National Association for Foreign Students Affairs, 1988).

Why Are You Leaving?

It is important to understand why you are going home. For some, whether you feel ready to go or not, there is no choice. Perhaps your assignment or that of your spouse is unexpectedly over—or in British parlance you are "made redundant." Maybe the country where you are working no longer welcomes you or your work. Because departure and reentry come quickly and unexpectedly, both can be unusually difficult.

More often you know that the job will eventually come to an end and you will have to return home, but this event has seemed so distant that you are not prepared when the time finally comes. This can be just as traumatic as the surprise departures.

Others leave because they choose to do so. Some are permanently resettling to retire or to live and work in their own culture. Others return temporarily—for the sake of the children's education, because they want to be near aging parents, or because the spouse wishes to pursue a career which has been put on hold during the years overseas. Some women, like Barbara, return home alone to pursue their careers, visiting frequently with their spouses working in a foreign post.

The reasons why one returns home have a great influence on one's adjustment to the home culture. People who have been forced to return home because the job no longer exists will find adjustment much harder than those who choose to return. Just as it is necessary to understand and appreciate motivations for going overseas in the first place, it is equally important to understand what brings you home.

How Have You Changed?

No matter how long you live in another culture, you become different people. If you can understand how you have changed, it will help you through the adjustments of returning home.

First, and most obvious, everyone in the family is at a different stage of development with different needs from when he or she left home. The toddler has become the ball-playing eight-year-old; the tearful ten-year-old is now a teenager; the husband and father has moved up the career ladder or will be taking up a totally new job or career; and you—partner, wife, mother, perhaps career person as well—may have changed most of all. If you have had household help overseas, you may not be sure that you are able to take care of your family as well as you could prior to your overseas move. But is your memory of what it was like before totally accurate? The ironing basket may have always overflowed!

You need also to assess if and how your values have changed. This assessment is important because it is usually reassuring; your most basic values, from honesty in relationships to the importance of nurturing and caring, do not change. What has changed is your awareness of the common concerns all people share, no matter where they were born or reared. Women the world over have ambitions for their children; they all yearn for a world where there is no war to kill their sons and daughters; they feel joy at the birth of a grandchild, and mourn the death of a loved one.

How you react to your overseas experience will affect how you view the return home and ultimately how you adjust. Those who hated living abroad and spent their days longing for home and seeking out only those places reminiscent of home may be surprised that they experience reentry shock at all. They will not expect to have any problems adjusting to home because they have done little else but dream about how wonderful it is. The reason for their shock is obvious. Their dream rarely matches reality and home fails to live up to their memories.

Those people who loved every minute of the overseas sojourn are also likely candidates for reentry shock, mainly because they have avoided thinking about returning home at all. Their reaction to home can be very negative as they constantly compare their home country and its people unfavorably with the wonderful place they have just left, remembering only the best parts of their overseas experience.

Those who find reentry less shocking walk a middle line. They appreciate where they have been and the changes which they have personally gone through. At the same time, they accept that they are now home again, where they understand the expectations and ways of behaving, even though they may no longer completely accept or appreciate them. They are able to retain what is important to them from each experience and to make a new life at home that synthesizes both.

How Has Home Changed?

What about your home country? How have it and its people changed while you have been gone? We use the United States as an example of a country that has gone through dramatic shifts. In his book, *Megatrends,* written in 1982, John Naisbitt reports on a Massachusetts Institute of Technology and Harvard University study, "The Nation's Families 1960–1990." Just a few facts from this study illustrate how those who have been overseas for much of the past two, five, or ten years are going to be bombarded with many differences in our society and the way it operates. We are not talking about passing fads such as hairstyles and fashion trends, but about fundamental changes. Here are some of his findings for the nineties:

> Husband and wife households with only one working spouse will account for only 14 percent of all households, compared with 43 percent in 1960. . . . Wives will contribute about 40 percent of family income, compared with 25 percent now [1982]. . . . At least 13 separate types of households will eclipse the conventional family, including categories such as "female headed, widowed, with children" and "male headed, previously married, with children." . . . More than a third of the couples first married in the 1970s will have divorced; more than a third

of the children born in the 1970s will have spent part of their childhood with a single parent.[2]

Perhaps the American trend which will affect us most is, as Naisbitt states, that "more than ever before people live alone. One in four is a single-person household, compared with one in ten in 1955." This is particularly startling, and disturbing, for those who have lived in countries where the extended family is the rule; universal marriage is still common; and children are the longed for, and expected, outcome of this union. How will your children react to those new friends who have been through the emotional trauma of a divorce and who may be living with one parent? Soon after Nancy's family returned to the States for a sabbatical year a few years ago, her son came home from school in tears because he feared his parents would get divorced just like everyone else's in his class.

Nancy points out the problems of establishing new relationships or renewing old ones for the returning American woman. While she has not been idle while overseas, she has often had the opportunity to work outside the home and follow other pursuits while the household work is done by others under her supervision. It does not take long to realize that home is not like that. Most American women juggle homemaking, careers, spouse, and children, and even manage to squeeze in a little time for exercise or a hobby. What may be hard for the returning sojourner is taking up old friendships or making new ones with women who have adapted to this new lifestyle. While there was plenty of time overseas to nourish friendships, at home it is often a case of "love to see you but I am so busy these days," which seems like a rebuff to the returnee who is not yet used to juggling her time.

The biggest change is the new status of women in the work force. Many returning women are faced with a combination of conflicting and confusing emotions about the current

---

[2] John Naisbitt, *Megatrends* (New York: William Morrow, 1982).

trends. Foremost is the feeling of being left out, or certainly behind. On the one hand, you are being told about all the women "achievers," big business executives. In a sequel to *Megatrends* entitled *Megatrends 2000,* Naisbitt and Patricia Aburdene write,

> Two decades after quietly preparing, gaining experience and being frustrated with the male establishment, women in business are on the verge of revolutionary change. Over the past two decades American women have taken two-thirds of the millions of new jobs created in the information era . . . . Now women are ready to break through the "glass ceiling," the invisible barrier that has kept them from the top . . . .[3]

On the other hand you hear about the failure of the women's liberation movement. Women are working and getting paid for it, but they are still not liberated. They are juggling, as we described earlier. In Great Britain there has been a backlash against the "superwoman" created by Shirley Conran. Women are realizing that they cannot do it all. As Eleanor Berman has said in her book, *Re-entering,*

> For many women the obstacles in returning to work are . . . the personal conflicts that are part of being a woman in an era of changing values. None of us are immune to these conflicts. We all hear the dual directives that women today receive—to be a caring, available wife and mother and the new one, to be an achieving, assertive career woman. Though it is possible to be both, it isn't easy, certainly not at the same time.[4]

---

[3] John Naisbitt and Patricia Aburdene, *Megatrends 2000* (New York: William Morrow, 1988); (London: Sidgwick and Jackson, 1990).

[4] Eleanor Berman, *Re-entering: Successful Back-to-Work Strategies for Women Seeking a Fresh Start* (New York: Crown Publishers, 1980). The career counseling section of this book is specific and helpful, as are the appendices on educational programs and financial aid, career information, and other references.

One of the major problems for women returning home from overseas wishing to continue their careers or go out to work at a new job is that their curriculum vitae or work resumes have a gaping blank for the number of years they have been abroad. Although they are encouraged to fill in any part-time or voluntary work they have done, somehow it does not seem as valid as the resumes of women who have moved up the ladder or followed a career path.

What Are the Stages of Reverse Culture Shock and What Effect Do They Have?

The stages of reverse culture shock are similar to those of culture shock, starting again with the honeymoon stage. Especially if you are returning from a developing country, you enjoy the luxury of water straight from the tap, fruits and vegetables that do not have to be soaked in some cleansing solution, one-stop shopping in the supermarket, and reliable utilities. When choosing a house, you do not have to consider whether there is a pump for the water, if the electricity works, or if there is a telephone. You do not have to buy a car from someone who is leaving but can go to a dealer and take your choice. The extended family is within easy reach, either by car or by telephone; you can again be part of all that is going on in the family and offer comfort and support.

But in a sense you become children again, just as you did when you first arrived in a new country. Many of your clues to how to behave have been lost; you do not understand the new fads; the supermarkets have expanded and contain prod-ucts you have never heard of; technology has moved on so fast you no longer know how the telephone system works. Eupho-ria fades when you start coping with practical details. You may become anxious, frustrated, even depressed when reality takes over.

The realities of home ownership become all too apparent. Overseas you had a landlord or an embassy to see to the repair of things; now you have to do it. Although it is wonderful to be near family, you now have to bear the responsibility of that closeness. Anxiety takes over and you long to return overseas. It does not help that few people in your home environment are interested in your life abroad. Many of them have only a vague sense of the rest of the world. The first question from neighbors may well be, "Haven't seen you for a long time, where have you been?" And when you tell them, the reply is, "Oh, it must have been fun, have you heard that Mrs. X had a baby?"

You move into the adjustment stage when you can accept that this is the situation and it cannot be changed. You can, however, remind yourself of what you came home to do and what you missed about home when you were overseas. Instead of thinking how impersonal the telephone is, start thinking what a time-saver it is. Barbara's husband, Peter, well remembers the first dinner party they went to after returning home and how surprised he was that the hostess kept leaving the table to go to the kitchen and returning with dishes of food. After a few minutes it sank in that they were no longer overseas with servants to cook and serve—at home, you did it yourself. You may also have to adjust to the fact that no one will pick up your dirty clothes and wash and iron them, mow the lawn, wash the car, or make the beds. You have adjusted when you come to the realization that you prefer the freedom to do things yourself, when and how you wish, and when the family has learned (or relearned) to do their share. You need to go slowly and make allowances, both for yourselves and others, when your expectations are not met.

Where Will You Settle?

You cannot expect your family to be settled in until you have a roof over your heads, transportation in place, the children in school, and the primary wage earner back at work. To reach this ideal state, you may have to make a number of decisions. Even if you are returning to familiar territory, things may have changed—schools, the situation at work, and community institutions.

You might be returning to your old neighborhood or village expecting it to be just as you left it two, five, or ten years ago. You could be in for a shock. Some small communities do not change much, but many have gone through profound changes, largely related to growth, and you may find it difficult to come to terms with new community systems and find your niche again. "All those new people have moved in and are running things" is a frequent complaint. There will be many questions, from the condition in which renters have left your rented home (or the availability of a new one), to changes in the school system, increases in the cost of living, and the current political climate. Probably you have kept in touch with one or two people who can help fill you in on all the changes and provide support while you find your way back into the community.

If you are going to a totally new place, all will be new, so you will have few, if any, specific expectations. You can prepare as if you were going to a new country, and you have become quite adept at that.

People who are retiring face a different situation. For people who have been living overseas for many years, it may be difficult to decide where home is. British friends faced this decision several years before retirement. They were both born in the Middle East; they met in Britain but did not live there very long; and they spent all their married life mainly in developing countries working for one of the U.N. agencies. Knowing that they did not wish to return to the countries of their birth and having little affinity with Britain after all the years overseas, they decided to settle in the European country in which their agency is headquartered. There they built a home and learned the new skills needed to live and work in that environment.

Some retirees from countries with cold climates opt to live in a warm country—Spain springs to mind. Retirees planning to return to their own countries sometimes buy property during a home leave, usually in a rush. These communities often emphasize leisure pursuits such as tennis, golf, bridge, and swimming. Many retirees, however, find this kind of atmosphere uncongenial and long for the vibrancy of the city. One of our friends who retired from USAID deliberately chose to settle in Washington, D.C., where she and her husband could stay in touch with what was going on. As she said, "We would have died in a retirement-type place with nothing to do but play and talk to people as old as ourselves." Some of the questions that those returning for retirement will want to consider are:

- Do you want to be near family?
- Do you or your spouse want to continue working, say as consultants to your previous employer? If so, you might want to live near the home office.
- Do you want to be accessible to friends, particularly those passing through with whom you used to work?
- Do you prefer urban or rural living? Bear in mind that rural life is often difficult when one becomes less mobile.
- What kind of climate do you want?
- How much house and garden do you want to take care of? Do you enjoy pottering in a garden or do you want to be able to leave at a moment's notice and just lock the door behind you?
- Do you want to live in a retirement community surrounded by people your own age?
- Most important of all, what do you want to do during your retirement years?

What Do You Face If You Return to Work?

Returning to a Job in the Home Office. If you are returning to work in the home office, you may be in for a difficult adjustment. If you have been your own boss or have been managing programs and people, suddenly finding yourself submerged in an organization with many interests and voices will be trying. Few are concerned about where you have been or how you can integrate your experience into the parent organization.

Some companies do not use their returnees well at all. This has been particularly true of North American companies that see their major markets at home and the international ones as secondary. They often treat the returnee as someone just back from vacation and fail to call on the skills and knowledge that have been acquired abroad. This is not always the case, however, as the global market becomes more important and foreign work experience assumes greater value.

For those reading this as they experience their overseas sojourn: maintain close contact with friends and colleagues at the home office who can keep you informed about the cross-currents of office politics. You'll be better prepared when you return. When you are back, connect with a strong support network of both those who stayed at home and others who have been abroad—it is unlikely that you are the only one in this situation.

Returning to a New Job—or Job Hunting. If you are returning because your job has ended with your present employer, looking for a new position is a priority. Often contacts made from abroad produce a "Send us your CV and drop in when you get back" response—not very positive but needing to be followed up. In some places, especially in the U.S., there are many support and job search groups for executives and middle managers. They can be helpful when you return to face the round of sending CVs, attending interviews, and finally, we hope, landing a new job. Executive placement services are also useful and can be contacted before you return so they can begin to investigate opportunities that might interest you. Being in touch with business organizations in the city or area you plan to move to should produce information about these kinds of services; professional organizations also have similar services and information.

You may be planning to join the ranks of the self-employed and become a telecommuter, that is, working from home with your telephone, fax, and personal computer. Barbara's husband chose this route, initially joining a small partnership as a means of finding his way back into the British scene and then striking out on his own in partnership with Barbara.

Return of the Trailing Spouse. If you have been a trailing spouse and have had to put your career on hold or been unable to upgrade your skills, you are probably eagerly waiting to pick up the reins again. Unfortunately, it is often much harder to reenter the job market or career ladder than you think.

Some of our friends have returned and found the ideal job immediately, only to realize after a few months that the juggling involved in being a wife, mother, and worker is more difficult than they had anticipated. Other women return home with unrealistic expectations. As one fifty-year-old friend told us, "I'm going back and getting a job. I really want to work." She had not worked for pay for twenty years, had a resume which did not emphasize her voluntary work sufficiently, and, worse, had only a vague idea of what she wanted to do. Six months after return she was no closer to finding a job and was very discouraged.

When constructing your resume, first write down everything you did abroad that used the skills you were trained in as well as your management and organizational capabilities. Ideally, you will have kept a running log as it is very difficult to reconstruct this information at the end of your overseas sojourn. It is also important to have obtained letters of recommendation as soon as you completed a job. Be sure to include organizing the Christmas bazaar, talks you have given to local groups or at the international school, and any work which can be documented as enhancing your skills, including your short stint with a development agency and the term on the school board. And be sure to list the new language(s) you have learned. In *The Relocating Spouse Portfolio,* Joan M. Pryce says,

One of the top priorities is putting together an employment portfolio of essential and useful documents which will save you valuable time when you arrive at your next post. . . . This complete and permanent composite of your work history becomes a cumulative record of accomplishments that will grow with each new job.[5]

When your list is complete, you may need help putting it together in a logical and attractive sequence, suitable for a resume or CV. If so, the help of a professional career counselor or resume writer will be invaluable. The expense of hiring a career counselor or entering a guidance program will be a good investment.

One friend was very eager to work when she returned but was not satisfied with the type of work she had been doing while overseas. She enrolled in a ten-month course in a new field which had interested her for some time. The course promised a job at the end for each graduate. There were times when she felt that taking the course at her age (forty-five) was a waste of time, but the resulting job opportunities proved to her that the investment in time and money was well worth it.

Many returnees want to use their overseas experience in finding work and seek jobs in fields that vary from development agencies to real estate. In cities such as Washington, D.C., real estate agencies employ returned expatriates who are advertised as people who really know what a returnee is going through. Relocation agencies are also keen to hire people who have been overseas and understand the problems.

You may not be able to find a job with development agencies, but you may find interesting work with projects designed to improve literacy, health, and welfare among the "third worlds" of your home country. Although it may seem discouraging, beginning as a volunteer in the right organiza-

---

[5] Joan M. Pryce, *The Relocating Spouse's Portfolio* (Washington, DC: Family Liaison Office, State Department, February, 1992).

tion can be a career boost. Women who work in women's health programs, for example, often put in time as a volunteer counselor in women's clinics before applying for a management position, thus giving credibility to their application. Whatever choices you make regarding your career, you will be making a "creative compromise," a phrase defined by Dr. Jacqueline Wexler, former president of Hunter College, as

> ... compromise that allows you to make the most of your situation at every stage of your life, realizing that no decision need be permanent, that we are always free to change and grow as our life situations, our need, our values change.[6]

For women trying to reenter the job market, these words should be put where they can be seen every day.

What Do You Need to Do for the Children?

The age at which children reenter (or in some cases, enter for the first time) their home country will obviously affect their success in adjusting. If they are school-age, the attitudes they have learned from their parents will also be a significant factor.

The single most important decision for children is where they will go to school. You will need to choose between a public ("state" in Britain) or private school. If you decide on the public/state system, find out the size of the school your children will attend. If they attended a relatively small school overseas (say 600–700 students) where they have had a lot of personal attention, they may be lost in a large urban school of three thousand. However, these schools often offer benefits such as a varied sports program, extracurricular activities, and a curriculum which offers many different courses. In the U.S.

---

[6] Jacqueline Wexler, as quoted in Berman, *Re-entering*.

a tracking system which puts accelerated students in smaller, more competitive classes may also exist.

Help is available to make decisions on schools, and some useful addresses are given at the end of the chapter.[7] Visiting schools when they are in session is always a good idea, if possible.

The major factor in the adjustment of children to reentry is a positive attitude, just as it is with their parents. With this, the children can weather the changes and difficulties which hit them at first—not knowing how to dress, who the latest "in" pop group is, the latest slang.

Often the dream of returning overseas can be a positive help in adjusting to home. We have a friend who returned to the United States at the age of sixteen. His prior exposures to that culture had been when he was one and ten. He did not want to return but had to because of family circumstances. At first he spoke about going back overseas constantly. His parents encouraged that goal even though they had no intention of going abroad again. They used his ambition as a prod to keep him going until he was comfortable at home. "You'll have to do well in this class if you want to go to college" and "You have to go to college if you want to go back overseas."

---

[7] Useful addresses for help with children: (1) for American foreign service families, AWAL (Around the World in a Lifetime), Family Liaison Office, Room 1216A, Department of State; (2) for information on schools outside of Washington D.C., contact the local school board; (3) for Britain, the *Independent Schools Guide* (ISIS), Murray House, 3 Vandon Street, London SW1H OAN or *The Guide to Independent Education* , Gabbitas-Thring Educational Trust, Broughton House, 6, 7 & 8 Sackville Street, London W1X 2BR; (4) for state schools, call the Education Authority of the county concerned; (5) for Global Nomads International, Norma McCaig, Executive Director, PO Box 9584, Washington, DC 20016; (6) for missionary kids, MuKappa International, 7500 West Camp Wisdom Road, Dallas, TX 75236.

Without realizing it, he began to adjust and, then, to appreciate the life around him. He never did go overseas again, but he made a successful reentry.

How Will Your Finances be Affected?

The return home often means a drastic change in your financial situation. No longer will your housing be paid for or school tuition fully or partially covered. Nor will you have use of a company vehicle and tax-free gas and many other perks. You may be faced with the financial burden of buying a house, a car or two, new clothes to better suit the climate, and paying full price for many goods which were cheap overseas. The carefully tended nest egg can be quickly wiped out. Many returnees find the struggle with money one of the most depressing and immediate aspects of adjustment.

Although the situation probably cannot be changed, you can plan for it, do some research on just what the expenses will be when you return, and try to set aside some reserve funds. You have to keep reminding yourself—and your family—that actually living in your home country will be much different from the periodic visits you have made over the past few years. Home leaves and the money one is willing to spend on them are not real life! The children particularly may take some time to realize that they cannot go out for a pizza several evenings a week or go on shopping sprees any time they wish.

What Records Will You Need?

In addition to thinking about and planning your return, it is necessary to gather pertinent records.You will need to collect and carry the following records with you just in case your luggage is lost.

- Letters of recommendation indicating work performed and skills exhibited

- School records—get all transcripts including standard-
  ized test scores
- Family medical records including write-ups of any significant or "exotic" (tropical) illnesses
- An inventory of everything in the luggage and freight
  and prices of goods purchased while overseas, as well
  as receipts.

What Do You Most Want to Do When You Get Home?

One special list to make before leaving is the things the
family is most looking forward to doing at home, as well as
the people and places they are eager to see again. In addition
to easing the pain of saying good-bye, the list will be a re-
minder of why you are glad to be home. Too often returnees
get so caught up in the routines of daily living that they forget
the things they were eager to do. Taking the time to do them,
even when it seems more important to buy a car or go to the
grocery store, can ease adjustment.

SAYING GOOD-BYE

Saying good-bye is often painful but it has to be done.
If you avoid it, you leave unfinished business, just as you may
have done when you first left home. This is the time to remember that many of the relationships you thought would end
have continued. This should give you courage to say good-bye
to people and places now, knowing that you will probably
meet again.

Some families have a pedantic but useful way of planning
their good-byes. They each make a list of people and places
they will miss and take the time to visit them. These times
become the special memories which make the first months of
adjustment at home easier.

Friends who are staying behind can help. One friend of
ours specializes in farewell parties. She makes up a guest list

with care to include friends to whom it may be hardest to say good-bye. She prepares a meal of the family's favorite local food. During the party she takes photographs. As a final send-off gift, she gives the family a book which includes the photographs, a brief description of the people there, and recipes for the dishes served. It makes a wonderful keepsake.

SIT BACK AND TAKE IT ALL IN

There are some sojourners who say preparations should be made for reentry from the first day you leave your own country. This is an extreme view and probably not wise. But it certainly makes it easier to come home if you have made the effort in the intervening years to keep in touch. If this has not been done, returning can be overwhelming, particularly for the children who may be complete strangers.

Do not fall into the group known as the "when we's." These people are constantly talking about their travels and adventures, oblivious to the raised eyebrows, sighs, and shrugs of indifference to events which happened ten thousand miles away. Strive to live in the present, especially if you move frequently. It is not productive to dream of the place you just left or to anticipate the next assignment. Grab the moment and get all you can from it. Treat your home country as just another overseas assignment. As is said in an insightful article on the subject,

> View the return . . . as a cultural experience. Be aware of how the "natives" live and use the special sensitivities gained from living overseas as a key to understanding yourself and [the country] better . . . don't expect too much . . . right away. . . . You, as well as your children, may need some time to catch up on . . . feeling comfortable once again back home.[8]

---

[8] Joel Wallach and Gale Metcalf, "The Hidden Problem of Re-entry," Denver, CO: *The Bridge: A Review of Cross-Cultural Affairs and International*

As you complete the cycle of your overseas sojourn with reentry to home, you need the same open-minded, interested attitude you had when you went overseas the first time. With this mindset, reentry can be the next exciting phase of a lifetime of new experiences.

Training (Winter, 1980). For more information on reentry see *Cross-Cultural Reentry: A Book of Readings*. Clyde Austin, ed. (Abilene, TX: Abilene Christian University Press, 1983).

thirteen

Managing Stress

Living overseas is a stressful experience even for individuals and families who make careful decisions and prepare for the transition. Stress is, therefore, a fact of life, something built-in, which must be dealt with in the normal course of living overseas.

The specific causes are many and consist of most if not all of the problem areas discussed in this book:

- The sudden encounter with so much that is new and different
- Culture shock
- The coincidental onset of a major life passage or transition
- The stereotypes your host nationals have of you
- Feelings of isolation and loneliness
- Disappointed expectations
- Communication problems, both verbal (linguistic) and nonverbal (cultural)
- The excessively long working hours your spouse may feel it necessary to put in
- The distance from home and the anticipation or actual arrival of bad news
- Your children's adjustment problems
- The dissatisfaction of not having the right job situation or no job at all
- Physical illness

• Feeling out of touch with your home and the world as you knew it.

Just listing them helps you appreciate the importance of developing skills in stress management.

WARNING SIGNS

Some of the most common signs that stress is getting to you are listed below. You might wish to mark for future reference those which tend to be your response to stress.

Anger Which Is Difficult to Control

Sometimes people find themselves flying into a rage at something which is so petty that unrestrained anger cannot be justified. Yet they are suddenly shouting and waving their arms, stomping their feet, and slamming doors. When they calm down and examine what caused the flash of anger, they are amazed at how trivial it was. They will probably also ask themselves if there was something else contributing to it. Uncontrolled anger can be a sign of stress caused by something that has little connection with the situation which actually sparked the outburst. One man confessed that he was so angered by traffic delays, he purposely drove his car into six full garbage cans—and got great satisfaction from the mess.

Excesses—Eating, Drinking, Smoking

Some people suddenly find they are drinking too much, eating anything in sight, or chain smoking. These excesses are often caused by stress. The party and dinner circuit allow us to slip too easily into dependence on alcohol to counteract the stresses imposed on us by a cold sober world.

Veterans of the foreign service are very much aware of the problem of excessive drinking. One U.S. Foreign Service officer, who became an alcoholic, wrote in an article in the *Foreign Service Journal* :

... alcoholism ... is an occupational hazard of a diplomatic career. While alcoholism is by no means unique to the Service, some of the causes of the disease—isolation, loneliness, stress— are endemic to Foreign Service life overseas, and frequently in large measure.[1]

It is hard *not* to drink to excess overseas, according to this author, who goes on to comment on the stigma attached to admitting that you have a problem.

The stigma of alcoholism worsens its effects. Overseas, where the line between private and professional life is rarely clear, families with a problem tend to keep it within the family. This unfortunately is especially true of alcoholism, which by its nature forces its victims into isolation.

When excesses occur, the individual must look for the underlying causes or stresses that provoke them. Drinking problems abroad are exacerbated by the lack of understanding and access to help in an overseas community.

Nervous Tensions

Many people find that stress causes tensions which affect everyday routines and behaviors. Some cannot concentrate, jumping from one thing to another in a haphazard fashion. They cannot complete a job or sometimes even a simple sentence. For others, sleep patterns change. They turn into escape sleepers who take naps morning and afternoon and then go to bed early at night. Others are insomniacs whose minds never want to shut off. They lie in bed thinking, never waking refreshed. They go into the next day tense and irritable from lack of sleep. A vicious cycle soon develops as more tension is added when they cannot finish appointed tasks.

---

[1] Anonymous,"Suggestion Box: Helping the Alcoholic," *Foreign Service Journal* 60, No. 2 (February, 1983): 22–23.

Others develop physical signs of tension. Tics or nervous twitches, shaking hands, or tremors in the legs are all outward signs. Too often concern focuses on visible symptoms rather than the root cause—stress.

Physical Illness

It is possible to become so tense that physical illness results—and the illness is real. Colds, flu, nausea, diarrhea—all may be experienced by the overstressed person. The illness has to be treated, but the reason behind the illness must also be found. Much has been written about healthy minds and healthy bodies and the correlation between feeling good about ourselves and staying well. Among the many women we know who live and work overseas, those who have a positive attitude about themselves and a basic enjoyment of what they are doing are rarely ill.

Illness is one way to drop out for a time when a situation becomes too much to handle. This happens often in families or individuals when they first move overseas. It is easy and acceptable to say to the world, "I have the flu and cannot come out today," rather than "I can't cope with anything today so I'm not coming out." A vague feeling of physical discomfort can become a real illness when you have enough time to think about it. It is important to recognize when illness is stress-related.

Withdrawal or Denial

It may be hard for some of us to understand how a person can withdraw from her life situation almost to the point of denying its existence, yet there are women who do just that. We asked a newcomer recently how things were going with household management. Her answer was that she managed the household by paying no attention to the help. While they went about their duties, she stayed in her room, not emerging until they were finished. She entered the kitchen only when she knew they were in their quarters for afternoon rest. She had withdrawn so completely that she actually tried to ignore three people who not only lived in her house but were responsible for her welfare.

Other women take refuge in recreational clubs or expatriate organizations where they can avoid meeting any but the most westernized of locals. They distance themselves from the local culture and take pains to maintain their own cultural aura around them at all times. Some seem almost to take a fierce pride in not speaking the local language and never going to any but the most westernized places.

Marital Problems

It is no secret that the stresses people experience both within marital and family relationships and as individuals vis-à-vis the rest of the world, often prove disruptive to the stability of a marriage. As with the stresses from other sources, pressures on a marriage may be aggravated or intensified in the overseas setting. Extreme care must be taken to distinguish stresses inherent in the marriage from those imposed upon it by living abroad.

More marriages do not end in separation or divorce overseas than in Britain and the United States, but when it happens overseas, marital breakdown can be much more difficult to sort out. As we have already pointed out, there are few supports for people with problems of any sort. Professional counseling is difficult or impossible to get, communities are small, secrets are impossible to keep, and gossip is rife. Couples who want to separate for a time to work things out find it difficult to do so when they are overseas. Women who are mainly homemakers overseas are more vulnerable and less likely to have a support system than their husbands, who at least may be able to rely on office colleagues for assistance. If a couple decides to get a divorce, the legal issues are much more complicated overseas, as are the economic issues.

Divorcing overseas is perhaps more painful than in a home setting. Most expatriate communities are family-centered, and people in the process of divorce can feel real alienation. There is no stigma attached to *being* divorced, but those in the process of *becoming so* can be made to feel uncomfortable.

An example is a couple of our acquaintance. They had two children. The wife went home during the summer, taking the youngest child with her. During the summer she decided to stay home and take up a new direction, so she broke her contract overseas (both partners worked) and left her husband and older child overseas. At such a distance (he was in the Far East and she in the United States), talking the problems through by telephone was both difficult and expensive, the children were worried by what was happening and by the fact that they could not see one of their parents, and the overseas community was more nosy than supportive. By the time the couple did meet, the gap was too wide to bridge and the marriage ended in divorce.

We state again that although divorce overseas is not more common, it is more difficult and more traumatic, especially for the children. Going overseas to give your marriage a new meaning is a wrong reason for relocating—the stresses of overseas living will only add to those of an already shaky relationship.

Depression

Depression takes many forms. Some women cry for no apparent reason; like the unrestrained anger, crying can be triggered by a trivial incident. Others stop communicating with new acquaintances while some bury themselves in books. One counsellor's first question to clients is "How many books did you read this week?" The answer is an indication of how depressed or withdrawn the client is. Still others spend inordinate amounts of time staying in touch with friends at home, leaving little time or emotional energy for meeting new friends and getting acquainted with the new environment. Some become morose, seeing nothing of joy or value in their new setting. They begin crossing off the days on the calendar until the golden moment when they can return home.

While this list of warning signs is by no means complete, it is a starting point. You may find it helpful to think back and identify signs of stress which you have experienced in the past, so that you can be alert to their possible recurrence overseas.

SUGGESTIONS FOR RELIEVING STRESS

What can you do when you find yourself under stress? How can you cope and turn stress energy into positive action? Here are some suggestions which have been helpful for other women.

Stocktaking

When you feel you are under a lot of stress, exhibiting perhaps some of the symptoms outlined above, it is time to sit down and take stock. Since taking stock means identifying the good and bad, the positive and negative in a situation, many have found that the following approach works, even though it may sound a bit pedantic. Make a list of the pros and cons of your life abroad. Begin by listing what makes you feel good about yourself. This should include anything from being in shape to more complex things like feeling good about mothering, being a supportive wife, or using your professional skills effectively.

Next, list what it is about the new situation which is difficult. Is there too much time with too few "right" things to do? Has your household help taken over tasks you would like to do? Have you lost some measure of personal worth because you do not have a job? Are they genuine or imagined adjustment problems your children are experiencing? Is not knowing the language driving you to distraction and limiting your mobility?

For each pro (positive) point, ask next how you can

maintain it as positive. Then, using that as a goal, determine the tools you need or the activities you can engage in which will enable you to accomplish your goal. For example, you are in shape and want to continue to stay in shape. Your list might begin like this:

Positive	To Maintain	To Accomplish
Feel good about weight	Need to exercise	Join health club
		Find exercise partners
		Learn new sport

Examine the negative aspects of your life in the same way. For each negative point, indicate what you might do to overcome it. Your list could begin like this:

Negative	To Overcome
Not knowing the local language limits my mobility and contacts	Study with a teacher X times a week
	Study lessons every day X hours
	Go to market twice a week to practice new words
	Join a conversation group

You may not be the kind of person for whom a simple exercise of this sort is helpful. Others, however, find it heightens their self-perception to move step by step through an exercise focused on their own attitudes and behaviors. In any event, if you are feeling under stress, it is important that you sit back and honestly take stock of what is happening. Too many women refuse to engage in a little self-examination and end up spending all their years overseas blaming the host country or countries for their unhappiness. It is essential to identify the stress points both within yourself and within the environment, and then work on those you can control.

In which areas can you most effectively maintain control of yourself or your situation? First of all, you can maintain control over your body. We believe that it is essential to keep in good physical shape and no one can really interfere in selecting the food you eat, the sports you engage in, and the weight you gain (or lose). There is no question that physical exercise relieves stress. This is true for two reasons. The actual physical act is relaxing. Also, if you exercise vigorously to maintain good health, you will automatically relieve pent-up tensions. You will feel better about yourself when you look in the mirror.

You can also maintain control over your mind and its improvement. We have suggested specific things to do elsewhere. Suggestions have also been made about other areas in which you can exercise control, such as in the use of your time and in the management of your household. The important thing is to exercise control wherever possible. It will help reduce the stresses you feel in the face of the uncontrollable and enable you to roll with the punches.

Learning Your Way Around

It is amazing how much stress can result from simply trying to find your way around unfamiliar streets at the mercy of a taxi driver you cannot understand. Feelings of being hopelessly lost, misled, or cheated make any trip pure torture. The cardinal rule for every newcomer is: learn your way around as soon as possible. Do it systematically. Get the best possible map and carry it with you everywhere you go. Explore outward from your home or office. See if it is possible to use drivers from the office to show you around the city.

Learning the culture, customs, and language are also part of learning your way around and will do wonders in combatting anxiety and stress. There is so much to learn at once that it may seem overwhelming. The only antidote to that feeling, however, is to take control of the learning process and do it systematically.

Move with the Rhythms of the Country and Relax

As we discussed earlier, Westerners become uneasy when time is wasted or, at least, is not spent doing something useful.

In many countries, time is conceived of differently and life moves at a slower pace. Moving with the rhythms of the country rather than trying to maintain the culturally based time orientation with which you have grown up can reduce your stress level dramatically. Do not expect all deadlines to be met. When they are, consider it a bonus.

Take time to relax, particularly during the busy settling-in period. In the weeks after arrival, you can push yourself to the brink of physical and emotional exhaustion. The desire to get settled and to start living is natural, but you need to take time out. Being overtired builds up stress, which is generally taken out on the first person who crosses your path—child, spouse, or household help. When your temperature starts to rise, take a break.

Make Time for Your Family

The social whirl which overtakes one in the expatriate community is breathtaking. Even when there is no special occasion, like Christmas or New Year, it is possible to go out every night of the week. The price paid for that sort of life can be high. One drawback is loss of family time. If you are an ordinary Western family, dinners at home are a time to be together, to reaffirm relationships and, in some cases, to contribute to the growth of the children. Another is sheer fatigue and a feeling of aimlessness—partying rarely gives one a sense of accomplishment and fulfillment. Ultimately, it is boring. The expatriate community is not all that large, so you see the same people over and over again. The gatherings cease to be special and become routine events.

Casual time with the children is particularly important. As parents know, children do not necessarily blurt out their problems at prescribed moments. They need plenty of informal occasions to make their feelings known.

Seek a Support Group and Work to Maintain It

We discussed the need for support groups earlier. The family is a major support group and is the first one to be strengthened and maintained. But there are needs which cannot be met within the family. In times of stress, a relationship with another person or group of people with whom you share a sense of kinship or special connection may be the key to getting over the hurdle.

On the other hand, avoid like the plague groups whose major purpose is to serve as a forum for the complaining of its members.

Taking Time to Remember Why You Have Come

There will be times when job uncertainties are great or when the family is having adjustment problems. At these times it is helpful to sit down together and reexamine your motives for coming and the goals you want to reach while you are abroad. Try to gain a perspective on the problems that you or other family members may be facing. You may find that you have got off track and need to reorder your priorities. Or you may discover that your original motives for coming overseas are not sufficient to sustain you during times of stress and that they need rethinking. Discuss the things you like about your new life and how you can emphasize them in your daily routines.

It may be that your goals are long-term and you are feeling stress because they are not being reached. Perhaps you are expecting too much. Transferring technologies, teaching new skills, establishing yourself in a profession, or learning a new culture or language are all long-range accomplishments. None will be accomplished in the first six months. You may be able to reduce your feelings of stress by setting some short-term or intermediate goals which can be reached more quickly and which will provide you with a needed sense of achievement.

Accept the fact that there will be gloomy days when nothing seems to come out right. Worrying about them will simply add to the stress. Try a pragmatic approach; when you feel down, find the things that are going well and concentrate on them; save the harder tasks for times when the gloom has lifted.

A Change of Scene

Vacations are an important part of your life—time to get away from it all. Many people who live overseas, for some strange reason, try to deny themselves these times away. They tote up their vacation days at the end of the year and proudly say that they have not taken one break. This practice is unhealthy; furthermore, most organizations do not really appreciate a person who is always on the job. Most corporations and agencies allow a generous amount of leave time and expect employees to take it. Take all vacation periods you are allowed and plan them with care. Allow plenty of time for relaxation. Some people feel that since they are overseas they should spend every holiday visiting some cultural or tourist site. If that relaxes you, fine; if not, do something else. Consider vacationing somewhere completely different from the place you live. If it is in a cold climate, go somewhere warm. If you are in a country where all food and water must be carefully treated before consumption, it is a luxury to vacation where these precautions can be thrown to the wind. Watch the happy face of your child as he sinks his teeth into an apple, skin and all!

Keep the needs of the whole family in mind when you choose a vacation spot. Find somewhere the children can roam undisturbed by stares or cheek-pinchers. Nancy's child blossomed on a vacation in Australia as he played on the beach unnoticed. He looked like everyone else for a change.

Indulge in luxuries that relieve you of the specific cares and worries inherent in your everyday life abroad.

Even if you cannot take an extended holiday, plan weekends that include a change of scene or routine. Two days in a cool mountain resort, or a boat trip along a scenic river or canal, free from household responsibilities, the typewriter and the schedule which ties you down, can lift the spirits and make everything look better—and it is one of the best ways to relieve stress.

Ask for Help

If you cannot deal with the problems which are causing stress in your life abroad, seek help as soon as possible. You may only need a skilled listener, such as a doctor, a pastor or a friend. In some expatriate communities there are counsellors and psychologists available; use them as resources for stress management. Pack your favorite book on stress-management techniques. You could be your own best therapist.

Remember, asking for help on problems arising out of the conditions of your life abroad is not an admission of failure in coping with life. The stresses experienced overseas are special and new and, perhaps most important, arise to a significant extent from unconscious conflicts between *your* attitudes, values, and habits of behavior and those of your host culture. Getting help in dealing with your problems is simply recognizing that the techniques you used in problem solving at home do not necessarily work as well overseas.

A Sense of Humor

We cannot emphasize enough the need for a sense of humor, particularly the ability to laugh at ourselves. Individuals who do not have this gift simply do not survive as well under stress as those who do. From the day you arrive funny things will happen, though they may not seem very funny at the time. Barbara had her first laugh during the unpacking process in her first overseas home. Out of a box containing pots and pans came two of the four wooden blocks which had been used back home to raise the kitchen table in order to accommodate her tall husband's legs. She conjured a vision of the tenants sitting at the sloping table, wondering about their peculiar landlords. In one of her moves, Nancy discovered the movers had packed bags of garbage and a batch of discarded toys intended for the Salvation Army.

You may have to work at getting the laughter going. Understanding the humor in a situation will probably not be as easy as it was at home, if only because of the language barriers (it takes a high degree of linguistic skill to "get the joke" in a foreign language).

Patty Patterson captured the point beautifully in a piece she wrote called "How to Do Yoga When You're Living in India":

> Put on loose-fitting, comfortable exercise clothing, get a towel or a small mat, and lie down on your back on the bedroom floor. Relax, go limp in the pose of the dead man. Breathe deeply, and let your mind go blank until you hear, "Madam! I'm sorry, Madam, gas cylinder is gone." Get up, with perfect control, put on dressing gown, telephone for new cylinder. Return to room, floor and begin again. If you lost your temper with the telephone, you must do extra rounds of breathing. Sit up, begin alternate nostril breathing. If you have inhaled eight counts through the left nostril correctly, you may wait to hear, knock! knock! "Madam! MADAM!" "What is it?" "Your tea, Madam." "Don't want any!" "Sorry, Madam, yesterday you took it." Go to the door, take the tea, and stick your tongue out, if you are feeling tense, in the facial lion pose. This has the effect of frightening your helper into his quarters, and it prevents aging lines.... Continue with more difficult postures. When you have achieved the head stand and are holding it, perfectly still, your reward will be, "Madam! Very sorry, Madam the dhobi has fallen from the roof!" "My God! Is he injured?" "No, Madam, fell very nice by reason of drinking." Sit calmly, let pictures form, watch them, but do not become

involved. . . . Soon you will become detached, and if you can ignore the odor of burning oil when you have just forbidden the cook to fry anything, you are on your way.[2]

---

[2] Patty Patterson, "A Long Walk Down a Short Pier, or Life in Delhi, Part 1: How to Do Yoga When You're Living in India," New Delhi: *United Nations Women's Association Bulletin* (1974).

Afterword

We hope that in our effort to provide practical guidelines for dealing with the problems one encounters overseas, we have not overemphasized the problems at the expense of the rewards. The rewards are in fact great. Living overseas can be, and for most people is, one of the most memorable and gratifying periods of their lives. We have not catalogued here the rewards, because it was not our intent. Yet, implicit in almost everything we have said is this message: living overseas is an exciting and enriching experience for the person who approaches it with a clear head and a flexible attitude. Even the problems are, for the most part, the other side of the coin to what is good and valuable in the experience.

There is so much to do and so much to learn when living abroad; there are so many new people to meet and new ways of life to observe. But there is more. Living overseas has what we call a "quality of dynamism" which can have a powerful and long-lasting effect.

This sense of dynamism comes primarily from the personal growth you experience living abroad. In dealing with the new and different, you grow and change, and this growth and change are in turn reinvested in the experience. Put differently, in the process of interacting with your new environment, you grow and change in ways which provide you with new perspectives which in turn further stimulate growth and change.

This dynamic quality hits you most strongly when you return home where, for many, life seems dull and routine, where an interest in the wider world you have lived in is almost nonexistent, where nothing seems to be *happening!* In retrospect, no matter where you were, whether it was chaotic or orderly, dirty or clean, noisy or quiet—it seems alive and vital in contrast.

The feeling was captured by Nancy's son one day shortly after they had returned from Egypt where the Cairo streets are frenetic if not wild and where Nancy experienced the worst (or the most exciting, depending on how you view those things) traffic conditions of all her time overseas. They were driving down the highway in Virginia when Michael's small voice piped up from the back seat, "What am I supposed to look at then?" he asked. There were no camels, no donkeys, no gesticulating drivers, no crowded buses, no sidewalk vendors—in short, nothing to *see*. He felt cheated.

There is always something to see when you live in a country and culture different from your own, and the seeing affects forever the way your eyes perceive the world.

Appendix A

Important Documents and Other Paperwork

Passports. Each family member needs a passport. Babies and small children should not be put on their parents' passports in case they ever need to travel alone or with someone other than their parents.

Immunization Records. An immunization record is required as part of the admittance procedure in many countries.

Wills. Do not leave the country without having an updated will on file. It should include directions on how to dispose of your property and on how to take care of the needs of your minor children. Leave a copy with your lawyer or a family member and take a copy with you.

Insurance Policies. Obtain health/accident insurance which covers international incidents and injuries incurred there.

Marriage License/Birth Certificates. Copies of birth certificates for all members of the family are often required. Also take a copy of your marriage license/divorce papers.

Traveler's Checks. Traveler's checks should be obtained in the names of all adult family members and should always be kept for easy access to funds in case of emergency.

International Driver's Licenses. Accompanied by a valid home-country license, an international driver's license allows you to drive in many countries while your local license is being processed.

Joint Checking Account. A joint checking account should be obtained in the home country to allow both of you access to funds whenever required.

Passport Photos. Carry an abundance of passport photos *and* the negative. They are required for registration forms and many other documents upon arrival.

Tax Papers. Take relevant tax papers to assist you in making yearly tax returns if you are required to do so.

School Records. If possible, obtain school records before you leave as this will be much easier than sending for them later. Get as much information as you possibly can that will assist new teachers in becoming acquainted with your child.

Power of Attorney. A power of attorney should be prepared to allow the spouse to act on behalf of the primary wage earner. Without this there are many countries which will not allow the spouse to dispose of personal property or export household effects. This becomes important if there is a death, divorce, incapacitating illness and possible medical evacuation, or other emergency evacuation requiring the spouse to clear the family affairs prior to departure. Check to see if this should be obtained in your home country before you depart.

Power of Attorney for the Children. To designate a medical establishment, a doctor or a friend to act on your behalf if your children need emergency treatment, a power of attorney is needed. For couples who travel and leave the children behind with friends, this power of attorney is essential both for the protection of the children and the responsible friend. Life-saving treatments will otherwise be delayed until the parents can be located.

Appendix B

United States Reciprocal Work Agreements

With some countries the U.S. has bilateral agreements which allow dependents to work. In other countries these are de facto arrangements which are more uncertain.[1]

A bilateral agreement " ... provides an expeditious procedure in which permission to work is granted almost automatically. There is no restriction on the type of employment that may be undertaken."

A de facto arrangement is " ... only an informal arrangement whereby a country allows U.S. dependents to work and the United States reciprocates. As there is nothing in writing, such an arrangement is subject to unpredictable change due to economic or political pressures, or even changes in personnel within a foreign ministry. It can be established or withdrawn at any time."

Countries with bilateral work agreements with the United States:

---

[1]Source: *Family Liason Office Quarterly* 1, no. 2 (April 1989).

Argentina
Australia
Bolivia
Botswana*
Brazil
Canada
Colombia
Denmark
El Salvador
France*
Grenada
Honduras

Israel
Jamaica
Liberia
The Netherlands
New Zealand
Norway
Peru
Philippines
Sweden
United Kingdom
Venezuela

*Limited number of dependents permitted to work.

Bibliography

Austin, Clyde N. *Cross-Cultural Reentry: An Annotated Bibliography.* Abilene, TX: Abilene Christian University Press, 1983.

——, ed. *Cross-Cultural Reentry: A Book of Readings.* Abilene, TX: Abilene Christian University Press, 1986.

Bastress, Francis. *The Relocating Spouse's Guide to Employment: Options and Strategies in the U.S. and Abroad.* Chevy Chase, MD: Woodley Publications, 1986. This book has a strong U.S. domestic bias; therefore, it is useful to women when they reenter the U.S. scene but not particularly helpful when they go overseas. There is a useful appendix, "Networks and Other Groups."

Berman, Eleanor. *Re-entering: Successful Back-to-Work Strategies for Women Seeking a Fresh Start.* New York: Crown Publishers, 1980. The career counseling segment of this book is specific and helpful, as are the appendices on educational programs, financial aid, career information, and other references. Women who qualify as "displaced homemakers" (someone with no work experience who has become responsible for her own support after a number of years at home) will find information on training programs, educational opportunities, and scholarships from Displaced Homemakers, Business and Professional Women's Foundation, 2012 Massachusetts Avenue N.W., Washington, DC 20036.

CBI Employee Relocation Council. *Relocation News.* A quarterly journal available to nonmembers: Centre Point, 103 New Oxford Street, London WC1A 1DU.

Darrow, Ken, and Brad Palmquist, eds. *Trans-Cultural Study Guide,* 2d ed. Palo Alto, CA: Volunteers in Asia, 1975.

Facknitz, Julianne Fraser. *Transitional Women: A Study in Cross-cultural Relations,* thesis. Goddard College, 1978.

Fouche, David. "Changing Places." *The Wings of AWAL* (April 1985).

Geneva Women's Cooperative. *With Our Consent?* Geneva: Geneva Women's Cooperative, 1983.

Gillespie, Peggy Roggenbuck, and Lynn Bechtel. *Less Stress in 30 Days: An Integrated Program for Relaxation*. New York: New American Library, 1986. A practical and easy-to-use book on dealing with stress.

Hall, Edward T. *The Silent Language*. New York: Doubleday, 1959.

———. *Beyond Culture*. New York: Anchor Books, 1976. A thought-provoking book on people's relationship to their culture.

Harris, Philip R., and Robert T. Moran. *Managing Cultural Differences*, 2d ed. Houston: Gulf Publishing, 1987.

Iyer, Pico. *Video Night in Kathmandu and Other Reports from the Not-So-Far East*. London: Black Swan, 1989. The author ". . . went to Asia . . . not only to see Asia, but also to see America from a different vantage point and with new eyes." In most places, America had arrived there before him.

Janssen, Gretchen. *Women on the Move: A Christian Perspective in Cross-Cultural Adaptation*. Yarmouth, ME: Intercultural Press, 1989.

Jhabvala, Ruth Prawer. *An Experience of India*. London: John Murray, 1966.

Kalb, Rosalind, and Anne Welch. *Moving Your Family Overseas*. Yarmouth, ME: Intercultural Press, 1992.

Kavanagh, P. J. *The Perfect Stranger*. London: Chatto and Windus, 1966.Written about his wife who died tragically young. It includes very perceptive sections about being an expatriate in Indonesia.

Kohls, L. Robert. *Survival Kit for Overseas Living: For Americans Planning to Live and Work Abroad*. Yarmouth, ME: Intercultural Press, 1984.

Lamb, David. *The Africans*. New York: Vintage Books, 1987.

McKay, Virginia. *Moving Abroad, A Guide to International Living*. Hong Kong, 1982. Available from VLM Enterprises, P.O. Box 7236, Wilmington, DE 19803.

Naisbitt, John. *Megatrends*. New York: William Morrow, 1982.

Naisbitt, John, and Patricia Aburdene. *Megatrends 2000*. New York: William Morrow, 1988; London: Sidgwick and Jackson, 1990.

Organization Resources Counselors, Europe, and Confederation of British Industries Employee Relocation Counsel. *Survey on Spouses/Partners and International Assignments*, vol. 2, London (19 January 1990).

Patterson, Patty. "A Long Walk Down a Short Pier, or Life in Delhi, Part 1: How to Do Yoga When You're Living in India," *United Nations Women's Association Bulletin*, 1974.

Piet-Pelon, Nancy J. "Reentry for Teens." *Foreign Service Journal* (June 1986).

Pryce, Joan M. *The Relocating Spouse's Portfolio*. Washington, DC: State Department (1992).

Pusch, Margaret , and Nessa Loewenthal. *Helping Them Home: A Guide for Leaders of Professional Integration and Reentry Workshops.* Washington, DC: NAFSA, 1988.

Romano, Dugan. *Intercultural Marriage.* Yarmouth, ME: Intercultural Press, 1988.

Stewart, Edward C., and Milton J. Bennett. *American Cultural Patterns: A Cross-Cultural Perspective,* rev. ed. Yarmouth, ME: Intercultural Press, 1991.

Storti, Craig. *The Art of Crossing Cultures.* Yarmouth, ME: Intercultural Press, 1990.

"Suggestion Box: Helping the Alcoholic." *Foreign Service Journal* 60, No. 2 (February 1983): 22–23.

Thayer, Nancy. *Stepping.* New York: Playboy Paperbacks, 1981.

Vandervelde, Maryanne. *The Changing Role of the Corporate Wife.* New York: Mecox Publishing Company, 1979.

Wallach, Joel, and Gayle Metcalf. "The Hidden Problem of Re-entry." *The Bridge: A Review of Cross-Cultural Affairs and International Training* (Winter 1980).

Werkman, Sidney. *Bringing Up Children Overseas: A Guide for Families.* New York: Basic Books, 1977.

Werner, David. *Where There Is No Doctor: A Village Health Care Handbook.* Palo Alto: The Hesperian Foundation, 1977. A very down-to-earth guide to dealing with health problems in remote areas.

About the Authors

Both Nancy Piet-Pelon and Barbara Hornby are particularly qualified to write about women living abroad. As professional women who have also been volunteers and homemakers, Nancy and Barbara know the challenges of adjusting to overseas living firsthand.

Nancy's first experience out of the U.S. occurred when she accompanied her husband to Indonesia. She has also lived in Bangladesh, Pakistan, Egypt, and Nepal. Nancy, who is a cross-cultural trainer and a population/family planning consultant, is now back in Bangladesh as Director of the Asia office of an international family planning organization.

Barbara's first cross-cultural experience took place in Britain, as the American wife of a Briton. She has also lived in India, Nepal, Indonesia, and Malawi. Barbara is an editor and writer and a partner in a human resources development consultancy and training organization.